READING
THE RABBIS

READING
THE RABBIS

The Talmud as Literature

David Kraemer

New York   Oxford
Oxford University Press
1996

Oxford University Press

Oxford   New York
Athens   Auckland   Bangkok   Bogota   Bombay
Buenos Aires   Calcutta   Cape Town   Dar es Salaam
Delhi   Florence   Hong Kong   Istanbul   Karachi
Kuala Lumpur   Madras   Madrid   Melbourne
Mexico City   Nairobi   Paris   Singapore
Taipei   Tokyo   Toronto

and associated companies in
Berlin   Ibadan

Copyright © 1996 by David Kraemer

Published by Oxford University Press, Inc.
198 Madison Avenue, New York, New York 10016

Oxford is a registered trademark of Oxford University Press, Inc.

Library of Congress Cataloging-in-Publication Data
Kraemer, David Charles.
Reading the rabbis : the Talmud as literature / David Kraemer.
p.   cm.
Includes bibliographical references.
ISBN 0-19-509623-1
1. Talmud—Criticism, interpretation, etc.   I. Title.
BM504.2.K688   1996
296.1'25066—dc20   95-20715

1 3 5 7 9 8 6 4 2

Printed in the United States of America
on acid-free paper

To Talia and Liviya,
two of the best readers I know

Preface

Over the course of the last decade, my scholarly interests have taken me in a variety of directions: first to the problem of writing an intellectual history of the Talmud (*The Mind of the Talmud*, 1990), then to canonical criticism of rabbinic literature, and then to another kind of religious-intellectual history of the rabbis of late antiquity (*Responses to Suffering in Classical Rabbinic Literature*, 1995). What united all of these projects, I have come to realize, is my interest in the Talmud as a literary document and, more particularly, *as literature*. In all of the works referred to above, as in others published in scholarly journals, I employed a method that was self-consciously literary, that is to say, which viewed the Talmud (and other rabbinic literature) as a composition which communicated as much through elements of style and fine-crafting as through the substance of what was written. But, with the exception of two articles published in the journal *Prooftexts*, I did not highlight the method I was using; the method served other ends. As a consequence, colleagues and students were not able to judge the method, nor try it out themselves. It is this condition that I attempt to remedy in the present volume.

My interest in the literary method began during my graduate career. At that time, I was taught to dissect the talmudic text, to deconstruct it into its composite sources. But as the sources were brought to the fore, the composite document was neglected, a condition that left me terribly dissatisfied. For reasons of temperament and the spirit of the time (critical literary studies being all the rage), I found myself far more interested in the whole than in the parts. I thus turned to the composite Talmud and sought to understand its composition.

Another factor also pointed me in the present direction. As I sought to begin the sorts of studies that interested me as an independent scholar (= no longer a graduate student), I found that certain preliminaries were necessary. If I wanted to write an intellectual history of the Talmud, I had to stake a claim for the nature of the evidence. What was this document before me? What could I know about its prehistory? What about its composition? Could I discover anything about its purpose? About its reception? To answer these questions—all necessary preliminaries to the work I hoped to do—I needed to compare and to judge available methods. What were the strengths and weaknesses of source-criticism? Of redaction-criticism? Of other methods of reading?

In the end, I have judged that the method which best withstands critique is one which views the text as a final composite whole. It is one which is attentive to the rhetoric and formularies of the text. It is one which recognizes that no text speaks for itself and that readers are always partners in the construction of literary meaning.

Many readers will already understand the disputes and issues I am hinting at. Others will find the details in Chapter 1. There I offer a defense of my reading the Talmud as literature and provide details of my chosen method and its consequences. I emphasize that reading the Talmud as literature does not exclude other readings. But neither should such an approach be neglected, for, I hope the reader will discover, it promises to uncover immense riches which other readings of the rabbinic corpus leave hidden.

In order for you, the reader, to judge the approach I am illustrating, you will have to be aware of what I mean when I speak of *reading* the Talmud. By speaking of "reading," I consciously seek to exclude the sort of overly detailed attentions which traditional yeshiva students brought to the text. They were (are) primarily concerned with the halakhic (= legal) implications of the Talmud and had little concern for its formulation as such. By "reading," I mean something closer to what we are accustomed to do when we read prose or fiction. But the Talmud does not permit this sort of free-flowing reading either. The Talmud stops the reader, beckons him or her to return to earlier points, interrupts the flow of reading. Accordingly, if you are to read along with me, you too will have to read the Talmud text slowly and carefully, being prepared to stop and review. I have included translations (my own) of the bulk of each text being read. To facilitate analysis, the translations are divided into individual statements or thoughts. These divisions are intended to reproduce what I consider natural divisions in text, but, of course, such judgments are subjective; different readers will sense different divisions. Thus, you must read through my breaks as well. What is crucial is that you take the time to read the primary text. Only then will you be able to judge the worth of my readings.

Because, as I said, I have been engaged in this work for years, I do not here begin from scratch. The chapters which follow bring together the fruits of earlier studies to which they are, one might say, intertextually related. Chapter 1, though mostly new, incorporates and updates parts of two earlier articles: "Composition and Meaning in the Bavli," *Prooftexts* 8:3 (September, 1988), 271–291; and "The Intended Reader as a Key to Interpreting the Bavli," *Prooftexts* 13:2 (May, 1993), 125–140. An earlier version of the analytical section of chapter 2 appeared in my "The Formation of Rabbinic Canon: Authority and Boundaries," *Journal of Biblical Literature* 110:4 (Winter, 1991); my earlier reading is expanded significantly here. Chapter 3 draws small parts of a reading I used for illustration in "The Intended Reader as a Key," mentioned earlier; the same is true of chapter 4. Chapter 5 builds on my reading of Eruvin 13b in *The Mind of the Talmud* (New York: Oxford University Press, 1990), pp. 141–146. Chapter 6 expands my analysis of Yevamot 13b–14b from "Composition and Meaning," mentioned above. And chapter 9 reproduces my extended analysis of Berakhot 5a–b, appearing first in my *Responses to Suffering in Classical Rabbinic Literature* (New York: Oxford University Press, 1995), pp. 188–200. Chapters 7, 8, and 10 are entirely new.

In view of the relationship of the present chapters to earlier publications, it will come as no surprise that readings in this volume benefit from the insights of several colleagues. I am particularly indebted to Alan Mintz and David Roskies, editors of *Prooftexts*, who, in my preparation of the articles which appeared in that journal, made important contributions and critiques. My appreciation of what it means to read the Talmud as literature gained immeasurably from my conversations with both of them, and I continue to be grateful for their wisdom and friendship. Jack Lightstone read chapters 2 through 9 and made important suggestions concerning the shape of my first and last chapters; I am grateful for the attentive reading of a scholar whom I respect and whose work I admire. Lori Lefkowitz read an earlier version of chapter 1 and suggested many essential critiques and improvements. The chapter is far better as a result of her input. Finally, I should mention that Burt Visotzky read an earlier version of chapter 10. Thanks to his good counsel, I abandoned that version and went with the present alternative.

I wish to thank Cynthia Read of Oxford University Press for her continuing support and friendship. She does a masterful job in an important position and the world of scholarly publishing is enriched by her attentions.

New York   D. K.
November 1995

Contents

Abbreviations

A.Z.	Avodah Zarah		M.Q.	Mo'ed Qatan
b.	Babylonian Talmud		Ned.	Nedarim
Ber.	Berakhot		Pes.	Pesahim
B.M.	Baba Mezia		Qid.	Qiddushin
B.Q.	Baba Qamma		Sanh.	Sanhedrin
Git.	Gittin		Shab.	Shabbat
Hag.	Hagigah		Sot.	Sotah
m.	Mishnah		Suk.	Sukkah
Mak.	Makkot		y.	Talmud Yerushalmi
Meg.	Megillah		Yeb.	Yebamot

READING
THE RABBIS

Introduction:
The Talmud as
Religious Literature

Early in my graduate career I participated in a Talmud seminar with David Weiss Halivni, considered by many to be the premier Talmudist of this generation. Halivni's method, a higher source-criticism, was directed at restoring the "original" (the quotation marks speak for my reservations, not his) version of traditions which, in his reading, had been corrupted in the course of transmission from one generation of rabbis to the next. Seminar time was devoted to identifying textual difficulties that were taken to be evidence of such corruptions and, through a combination of comparison with parallel texts and intuitive speculation, suggesting the "urtext" from which the tradition at hand had derived.

Debate often focused on the question of which sorts of considerations could properly be brought to bear on the project of restoration. Reduced to its starkest elements, the debate was this: Was the Talmudic tradition we were studying a legal one, in which questions of the law and its rational limits constrained all possibilities, or were matters of formulation, balance, and the like also at play? Would the rabbis formulate traditions that made less legal sense but were stylistically more elegant or functional (= easier to memorize)? Or, to put it in the words of one participant in the seminar, was the Talmud we were studying "Law or Literature?"[1]

The considerations Halivni brought to bear certainly seemed "literary"—words could appear in a tradition merely for stylistic balance, and sometimes such matters of formulation could be given priority over legal rigor. But as the discussion progressed and questions of the "literary" qualities of the Talmud arose time and again, no one ever bothered to ask what we meant by literature. Nor did anyone ask how the Talmud's "literariness," if it was present at all, might affect the way we were reading it. It was as though everyone knew, or at least intuited, what this all meant. As a consequence, we barely defined a method. We proceeded, sometimes with genuinely brilliant outcomes but more often with highly subjective results, more on the basis of intuition than on the foundation of a self-conscious method.

We were not the first to have proceeded in this way, nor the last. In 1962, Avraham Weiss published a book, *On the Literary Production of the Amoraim* (the latter are the named sages in the Talmud), in which he examined the history of the development of the Talmud's basic rhetorical unit, the sugya.[2] In his extended consideration, "literary" meant attention to questions of ordering—though he never defined what he meant by literary nor, again, what difference viewing the Talmud as literature would make. Much later, Jacob Neusner and his students published a critical volume (entitled "Law as Literature") on the work of Halivni, Shamma Friedman, and Weiss, but, again, no definitions.[3] The same is true of the recent work of Louis Jacobs, in which "literary" means both "ordered" and (often) "contrived."[4] Still, no definitions and no consideration of the difference "literary" makes. This absence of methodological consciousness has led to anemic results, and thus, even with these efforts, we are now hardly closer to knowing what it might mean to read the Talmud as literature than we were previously. My intent in this volume is to begin redressing this condition.

Let us commence, then, with the fundamental questions: Is there a generally accepted definition of "literature" and, if there is, can the Talmud be said to be literature according to this or any other supportable definition?

As even readers who have only "dabbled" in contemporary literary studies will know, the scholarship relating to the question "What is literature?" is vast, and it is well beyond the scope of this brief introduction to evaluate the state of the field. For present purposes, therefore, I choose two pertinent discussions, essentially at random. I justify this approach by reference to my conclusion, in which I reject the possibility of a commonly accepted formal definition of literature. It makes little difference, therefore, with which particular definition we begin.

The discussion of René Wellek, in the classic work of New Criticism, *Theory of Literature*, considers a variety of definitions, from "everything in print" to "great books" to "imaginative writing." In conclusion, the author proposes that literature be defined as that species of imaginative writing which uses language in a particular way. In his words,

> literary language . . . abounds in ambiguities . . . it is highly 'connotative' . . . it has its expressive side; it conveys the tone and attitude of the speaker or writer . . . it also wants to influence the attitude of the reader, persuade him, and ultimately change him.[5]

Wellek goes on to admit the frequent difficulty of distinguishing between literary language and other languages, but his conclusion is a confident one. Despite difficulties, through a combination of characteristics, literature reveals itself clearly to the knowing reader.

In his *Literary Theory: An Introduction*, the Marxist critic, Terry Eagleton, assembles a similar parade of possible definitions.[6] In addition to those possibilities reviewed by Wellek, Eagleton adds " 'nonpragmatic' discourse," a discourse which employs "*self-referential* language."[7] But he rejects this definition, along with the others before it, as less objective than they claim; in all cases, it is too easy to point to exceptions or problematic examples. Instead, he in the end affirms the very subjectivity which undermines other attempts at definition. Literature is, in Eagleton's opinion, "any kind of writing which for some reason or another somebody values highly"; that is, "If they decide that you are literature then it seems that you are, irrespective of what you thought you were." Therefore, literature (or literariness) is not essential to the work but a function of how that work is read. In Eagleton's example, "If I pore over the railway timetable not to discover a train connection but to stimulate in myself general reflections on the speed and complexity of modern existence, then I might be said to be reading it as literature."[8] In other words, "literary" is a lens one chooses, not a characteristic of the text on which the reader focuses that lens.

For the sake of argument, let us, for a moment, "accept" each of the suggested definitions and consider how the Talmud measures up against each. If literature is "great books" (Wellek and Warren, p. 21), then a case can certainly be made that the Talmud is such literature. Few works have survived for so many generations, with so much sustained attention. If literature is properly "imaginative literature" (ibid., p. 22), then again the case can be made—any student of the Talmud knows how often its deliberations have little to do with an external reality. It is also clear that the Talmud uses language in specific and peculiar ways, ways it cannot have been used by common ancient speakers of Aramaic. The Talmud's language abounds in ambiguities, is highly expressive, and clearly wants to "influence the attitude of the reader." Whichever formal definition we adopt, it is not difficult or unreasonable to argue that the Talmud is indeed literature.

Yet, we must admit, the Talmud is not what people commonly mean when they speak of literature, and this is precisely the problem we must overcome before we can proceed. How can the Talmud be literature (or literary) and not literature (not literary) at the same time? The solution, I believe, lies in our recognition that "literature" is being used in these discussions—often without sufficient consciousness—in two distinct ways. "Literature" is, on the one hand, something like "everything in print" or, to be somewhat less extreme, everything of import and accepted merit in print. In this usage, "literature" designates a large category with innumerable subgenres (legal literature, poetry, biography, historical literature, novel, myth, etc.). On the other hand, literature is belles lettres, and, in this usage, "literature" is a subcategory of literature. In other words, just as there is legal literature and historical literature, so too is there "literary" literature, which includes novels and poetry but may or may not include myth (depending upon how one defines the subcategory "literature").

This distinction may be illustrated by reference to two distinct— and chronologically distant—discussions of the Bible as literature by Northrop Frye. In *The Great Code: The Bible and Literature*[9] (not "The Bible as Literature," the author emphatically notes), Frye writes that "the Bible is not primarily literary in intention" and, later, that "the Bible seems not to be literature though it has all the characteristics of literature."[10] Yet, several decades earlier, in *Anatomy of Criticism*, Frye wrote "the Bible is a work of literature as long as it is being examined by a literary critic."[11] How may this apparent contradiction be resolved? In *The Great Code*, I think, Frye is using the term "literature" to designate a genre. How else could the Bible not be literature and yet have all of the characteristics of literature? Clearly, formal, structural characteristics cannot define "literature" in this usage. Rather, "literature" is here what Ellen Schauber and Ellen Spolsky call a "functional genre,"[12] a genre defined primarily by its function or purpose and not by its form. So, in Frye's estimation, the Bible is not intended to serve as literature. Yet its qualities are literary nonetheless. Crucially, even when Frye thinks the Bible is not literature, in the more limited sense, he sees fit to read the Bible as a literary critic. We shall return to this point later.

Rejecting the possibility of offering a single, limited definition of literature, we are better off positing that the Talmud *is* literature and asking what genre of literature it is. Yet, here, too, we confront immediate difficulties. Genre definition is a matter of comparison and contrast: What other literature is this literature like and in what ways is it different? Frye's discussion of the Bible as literature but not literature shows the difficulty of this task. With respect to a work like the Talmud, the difficulties are perhaps insurmountable. Certain observations may readily be made: The Talmud is not a novel (though it may often be fictional). It is not poetry (though it may sometimes strike the experienced reader as poetic). It is not story (though it contains stories); it is not myth or folktale (thought it contains each); and it is not history (though it sometimes claims to relate historical narratives). But other suggestions for the Talmud's genre are less clearly supported or rejected. The Talmud is in some sense legal literature, but it is not a law code, and it contains ample quantities of material that we would not find in other legal literatures. The Talmud is in some respects a commentary, but it looks unlike any other commentary known to me (even within the Jewish tradition). It is religious literature. It is philosophical literature. Each of these designations can be supported, yet the Talmud can also be shown to be different, in significant ways, from other works of literature which are assigned to these genres.

The work to which the Bavli is most similar (though there also remain notable differences) is its sister Talmud, the Yerushalmi. Yet if, to avoid problems, we assign the Bavli to the genre of literature designated by the term "talmud," we have merely formulated a great tautology (the Talmud is talmud). It may indeed be the case that the two Talmuds constitute their own genre. But, by itself, this observation advances us very little. What does talmud mean? What are its purposes? What are its assumptions? The tautological definition answers none of these essential interpretive questions.

There will be some experienced students of Talmud who will argue, to the contrary, that once they have identified a text as talmud (=genre) they will know just how to interpret it. In my view, this confidence is naive. The Talmud is an ancient document, one that has been studied by generations of Jewish males over the last many centuries. Those generations have developed their own understandings of the Talmud's methods and purposes, understandings conditioned by the times and conditions of the readers. Surely, we can say with considerable confidence how the genre "talmud" was understood in recent Yeshiva culture. But if we put aside the long interpretive tradition, we are left with an ancient text and, as even E. D. Hirsch Jr. admits, the more distant we are from the time and place of a text's composition, the more difficult it will be to recover the "cultural givens" necessary to understand it.[13] Later interpretive prejudices are part of our immediate inheritance. The assumptions of the ancient authorship and its readership are probably beyond our reach.

Yet if, as Hirsch claims (and I agree), "All understanding of verbal meaning is genre-bound"—that is to say, our interpretations of a text are strongly predetermined by what we expect to find in it—then our inability to define a genre for Talmud beyond the limited, imprecise, and chronologically and culturally distant designation "talmud" leaves us in a quandary.[14] It leaves us, literally, without a place to begin. To escape this quandary, we must abandon hope of suggesting a fully satisfactory definition for the genre "talmud" and admit, instead, that any genre definition is imperfect, unstable, and the product of prejudice (prior judgment). By putting such a hope behind us, we may turn instead to less perfect but more fruitful genre comparisons and thereby permit ourselves to commence reading.

The most important step we can take (as suggested earlier) is to recognize that, whatever its more particular genre, talmud may be viewed as a genre of literature. But what does it mean to claim that the Talmud, which is not literature in the commonly recognized sense, is nevertheless literature? In his essay "Theory of Genres," Frye asserted that "the Bible is a work of literature as long as it is being examined by a literary critic." Indeed, in *The Great Code*, Frye demonstrates what it means to read what he calls "not . . . literature" as literature.

In this exercise, Frye confirms in practice Eagleton's assertion, quoted earlier, that even a railway timetable may be read as literature (though, to be sure, it is easier to do this with the Bible than with a railway timetable or a phone book). Ultimately, both critics agree (despite significant differences in their theoretical assumptions!) that literature is as much a way of reading as it is an objective characteristic of any particular form of writing.

If "literary" and "literature" are a product of the lens one uses, then any genre of literature may be read, and fruitfully interpreted, through a literary lens. The Bible, literature or not, may be read and interpreted as literature. The Talmud, literature or not, may similarly be read as literature. Because literature is defined by a way of reading, erecting barriers between "literature" and other kinds of writing serves little purpose except to define academic departments. On the contrary, the insights of those who study and interpret literature well serve those who study other writings. Thus, as Frye demonstrates, the readings of a literary critic contribute abundantly to possible understandings of the Bible. And the questions of critical literary studies have been brought to bear on contemporary legal studies with great profit.[15] Our question, therefore, can no longer be whether the Talmud is literature (it is if we read it as such) or what genre of literature it is (it doesn't matter) but what questions, insights, and observations the reader of literature brings to bear on the literature which she or he reads.

What, then, are the "literary" questions? What is the lens we must employ if we are to read the Talmud as literature?

We begin, surely, with the fundamental question of all interpretation: What does the text mean? To get at this meaning, we consider many of the factors that others before us have rightly intuited: How is the text formulated? How does its ordering affect its sense? Are certain common conventions followed, and to what end? Is there hyperbole? Where is the text realistic and where fantastic? And so forth.

But these questions are a mere beginning. By themselves, they fail to define a literary approach. As employed by those scholars spoken of earlier, these questions have often (even primarily) been applied to isolated traditions or strings of traditions.[16] The interest of those who ask these questions has been to atomize the Talmudic text, employing "literary" criteria for source-critical ends. But the concern of the reader of literature is to comprehend the meanings of the text at the level of its final composition. This should be true for the Talmud as much as for any other piece of literature. Whether a source-critical history of the Talmud can or cannot be written is a question scholars will continue to debate. But, whatever the fate of this question, one thing is clear: the Talmud is a text in which the "redactor's"—more correctly, *author's* (I assume that there were multiple authors)—hand remains always at or close to the surface. Whatever the sources from which he draws, the author actively shapes his sources to create a composite whole. Thus, the Talmud too demands a literary reading, in which "literary" means attention to the composition as we preserve it. For what purpose was the text put together in this way? How does its arrangement impact upon the reader to create a meaningful impression? How are rhetorical turns employed to affect the development of a thesis? What in the synthesis of the parts into a whole influences the reader's understanding of the composite message?

But reading the Talmud as a finished literature does not mean ignoring the "sources" it quotes. On the contrary, these "sources" are an essential part of the Talmud's rhetoric. The undeniable fact is that the gemara's vocabulary is not merely independent terms or phrases, but whole units of opinion or discourse attributed to earlier authorities. We must also ask, therefore, how the compositional shaping of tannaitic and amoraic traditions creates a new statement of meaning. This is particularly true because the author often appears to change the "original" meanings of the traditions he quotes; that is to say, the reader's sense of the meaning of a tradition will often differ from the meaning claimed by the gemara. How, then, does the author's choice and arrangement of earlier traditions affect our understanding? How does his shaping of source materials create a coherent thesis? What is the nature and authority of his sources and proofs? Is his logic cogent, or are there contradictions? All of these questions, too, are demanded of the Bavli's reader.

But even these will not be enough. Recognizing that interpretation is an imprecise and highly subjective process of readings and rereadings, we must enter the hermeneutic circle and admit its circularity. Interpretation, in its very nature, proceeds in fits and starts. No two readers can or will follow precisely the same steps. For this reason, we are obliged to ask the question that has detained literary critics perhaps more than any other in recent years: What is the place of the author in the creation of meaning and what the place of the reader? By saying that we want to know what the text *means*, are we really saying that we seek to determine the author's intent? And, even if this is what we hope to achieve, to what degree does the process of reading and interpreting allow for this determination? Or, stated simply, is the meaning of a text determined by the author, constructed by the reader, or the product of the interplay between them?

Some critics continue to maintain that meaning is controlled by the text (this paradigm has surely dominated in Talmudic studies). Others, in recent years, have argued that meaning is the construct of a reader. Though, as a matter of theory, I lean in the latter direction, it seems to me reasonable, in practice, to locate the construction of meaning somewhere between these two extremes. The formulation of Owen Fiss suggests a practical balance: "Interpretation, whether it be in the law or literary domains, is neither a wholly discretionary nor a wholly mechanical activity. It is a dynamic interaction between reader and text, and meaning the product of that interaction."[17]

Anyone who has written knows that an author intends to communicate a particular meaning. The author will choose her language as carefully as possible to communicate that meaning. Of course, such communication is, by definition, two-sided. The author directs her writing at an audience, at an intended reader. An author composes by choosing literary signals (her rhetoric) which she hopes will communicate effectively to that reader. In making her choices, she recognizes (if only intuitively) that what a signal means to one kind of reader it will not mean to another. Thus, she selects signals that are appropriate to the intended reader. The more skillful the author, the more successful she will be at directing the reader's reading and, therefore, at determining the meaning communicated.

But, as anyone who has published also knows, once a work is published, the author gives up control of meaning and various readers make determinations about what the text means. Surely the author's words do influence the reader's understanding. When all is said and done, however, it is the reader who understands the text as he understands it—not perfectly and completely, as the author would have liked it to be understood.

Critics are readers. Interpretation of any literature is never, therefore, an objective act, but neither is it arbitrary. The critic may ask what a text means or what an author intends, but only if he makes claims for interpretation modestly—with recognition of the necessary limits of all interpretation—and only if he accounts for the place of the reader in constructing the meaning of a text. For those of us who seek to interpret ancient texts and recapture, to the extent possible, the intention of the authors of those texts, this means we must imagine the reader whom the ancient author intended to address. If we, as readers, assume the position of the intended ancient reader, then we will be better placed to read the author's communication as he intended. We will still be limited by the imprecisions of any interpretation, and we will never perfectly perform the translation of ancient reader to modern. But we will at least be closer to the mark for which the ancient author aimed.

In the case of the literature at hand, the Bavli, critical attention to the role of the intended reader is especially crucial. The Bavli's authorship fashioned a work that constantly demands the reader's contribution to its final communication. The Talmud is replete with ellipses and other gaps, its arguments often build on unstated logical associations or contrasts, and it routinely addresses the reader directly (to list only a few of many characteristic strategies). Roy Kreitner puts it this way: "As far as the Bavli's internal workings are concerned, the structure and content of the document force *reader intervention* in the text, cancelling the possibility of a passive reader."[18] Clearly, by choosing to express themselves this way, the Bavli's authors anticipated that "*talmud*" would be the product of a dialogue between text and reader. For this dialogue to progress as intended, a certain kind of reader would be necessary, and the authors surely had a vision of this reader. To interpret their intent, therefore, we must first attempt to capture their vision.

Who, then, was the Bavli's intended reader? Certainly, he lived and studied in sixth-century Babylonia.[19] The evidence of the text itself shows that he was a member of a schooled elite who understood scripture in its original language, committed much of scripture to memory, and was able to apply certain specialized methods to its interpretation. He also commanded significant quantities of the Mishnah and related texts. Indeed, it is safe to say that even to begin studying the Bavli's deliberation, the reader needed to have devoted a significant number of years to acquiring command of the rabbinic tradition. Our reader was, at the very least, an advanced rabbinic disciple.

The Bavli's routine demands show that, in addition to significant technical preparation, its intended reader also required considerable ingenuity and intellectual prowess. The following text, discussing restitution for the improper consumption of produce set aside for priests *(terumah)*, will illustrate the point.

Yebamot 90a

a. [Objecting to the claim that the rabbis do not have the power to uproot regulations of the Torah] Come and hear [what is taught in a beraita]:

b. If he ate *impure* Terumah, he [must re-]pay *pure* common produce. If he paid *im*pure common produce, Symmachus says in the name of R. Meir: If unintentionally, his repayment is payment; if intentionally, his repayment is not payment. . . .

c. And we deliberate on it—

d. "If intentionally, his repayment is not payment"?! [On the contrary,] may blessing come upon him, for he ate something that was not fit for him [the Priest] in the days of his impurity and paid him something that was fit for him in the days of his impurity.

e. And Rava said [in response to this objection] . . . The text is flawed, and this is what should be taught:

f. . . . If he ate *pure* Terumah, he pays *pure* common produce. If he paid *im*pure common produce, Symmachus said in the name of R. Meir: If unintentionally, his repayment is payment; if intentionally, his repayment is not payment. . . .

g. And here [if he intentionally repays impure common produce] his repayment *is*, according to the Torah, proper repayment . . . yet the sages [= R. Meir] say, "his repayment *is not* payment". . . . [emphases added]

As you have no doubt already felt, the demands this text makes upon a reader are enormous. Aside from a considerable store of knowledge concerning the laws of priestly gifts, purity and impurity, and so forth, the text requires that the reader command several complicated steps of deliberation (a–f) before the major point—the objection—may even be articulated (in g). Anything less than the most rigorous and capable mind might be forced to abandon this pursuit before the goal is reached. Yet, though this objection is longer than many, it is in no way exceptional. The difficulty of this text bespeaks volumes concerning the document's assumed reader.

What of the reader's critical propensities? Roy Kreitner writes, "[the Bavli's] technique . . . brings to light incongruities (the unharmonious) in the sources and the heterogeneity of the evidence . . . the mode of address assumes a constant critic (the reader), paying very close attention." [20] The Bavli models, and insists that its reader participate in, the critical exercise of comparing sources, contrasting logics, and seeking inconsistencies. It offers competitive interpretations and demands that the reader evaluate them both against one another and against his own sense of the meaning of a text. It demonstrates, through the very comments it makes, that the approved stance with relation to a source-text is not to receive it passively, but to question, object, and otherwise respond critically. The reader never abandons his own judgment; on the contrary, he is asked to use his judgment to advance the deliberation.

A sugya at Yebamot 91b well illustrates the assumed critical nature of the reader. The text discusses whether the claim "What could she have done?!" *(mai havei la lemiaʿvad?)* may be used to relieve a woman of penalties after she has unwittingly become involved in a prohibited relationship (such as when witnesses have incorrectly testified that her husband is dead, whereupon she remarries). Six Mishnahs that appear to suggest that such a defense is not available to her are quoted. However, all are followed by responses that explain that in each case she could have done something to avoid the prohibited involvement. Thus, the quoted Mishnahs are not relevant to the question at hand. Though not all of the responses are likely to satisfy our sense of what is reasonable, they are no more or less strained than similar responses found throughout the Bavli.

At this point, the gemara records the following exchange:

a. R. Pappa intended to render a judgment based upon the principle "What could she have done?!"
b. R. Huna the son of R. Joshua said to R. Pappa: But have we not taught all of these Mishnahs [which suggest that this principle may not be employed]?
c. He said to him: And have they not been explained [showing that they are not relevant]?
d. He said to him: *And should one depend upon [mere] responses/ explanations?!* *(veʾashinuyei leiqu velismokh?!)* [emphasis added]

R. Pappa, and the reader with him, is called upon to judge the strength and coherence of the gemara's responses. Formally, they all "work" (as will such responses throughout the Bavli). But formal success does not eliminate the obligation to examine critically. No reader understanding the model offered in this exchange will assume that responses or resolutions are to be accepted without question. On the contrary, even apparently successful resolutions are, in the eyes of the Bavli, appropriately subjected to the reader's critique.

Based upon what we have seen, we may first reaffirm the obvious, that is, that the Bavli's intended reader was a Jewish male of considerable intelligence and advanced rabbinic training. But we may now also add other less-expected qualities: The reader whom the Talmud addressed was confident and critical, capable of grasping the most sophisticated analyses and arguments and predisposed to evaluating each from a variety of perspectives. Like the Bavli itself, he challenged and questioned, and he was anything but intellectually submissive. His piety did not demand simple acceptance of received traditions. Instead, he was called upon (intellectually, at least) to transform the tradition according to his own reasoned understanding. He was the incumbent master of a developing tradition, one which he had a hand in transforming.

This characterization of the Bavli's intended reader has one important consequence for the readings that follow in subsequent chapters. If the Bavli speaks to a restricted, elite society, this means that, however we are tempted to interpret its ideologies and messages, we must be mindful that it is not a popular communication. Of course, certain messages that might appear threatening or radical if offered before a popular audience would not be so if shared in the restricted society of colleagues. The same claim that would provoke a defensive response if articulated by an outsider could invite welcoming curiosity if spoken instead by an insider; and the Bavli is talking in the company of insiders. We should thus be extremely cautious before responding, "the Bavli couldn't possibly be saying that!" (where "that" is an opinion that contradicts our sense of common Jewish piety). The Bavli *could* be saying "that," though it might not intend to share "that" with more than a relatively small number of like-minded Jews.

Having accounted, then, for the place of the reader, I am finally prepared to describe fully what I mean by reading the Talmud as literature.

Reading the Talmud, as reading any literature, is a process, demanding the constant interventions of the reader. We would be mistaken, therefore, to ask what the Talmudic text "says." The text does not say anything complete and coherent in the absence of its reader. Accordingly, our attention must also turn to the reader before we venture an interpretation of any given Talmudic deliberation. Ideally, we should put ourselves in the place of the intended reader; otherwise we will be unable to imagine the voice that completes the Talmud's discourse. The Talmud's contextual communication requires that we remake ourselves, as much as possible, in the image of the Talmud's intended student. Only then will we stand a chance of approaching (though never capturing) the author's intended message.

Having assumed, to the best of our ability, the position of that intended reader, we must undertake the task of interpretation as would any such reader—over time. A reader, in dialogue with the text he reads, doesn't create meaning in a single static instant. He reacts to a text by formulating preliminary interpretations and then, under the pressure of additional information, formulating revised interpretations. These reinterpretations, and their accumulated impact, have meaning. The recognition that Talmud is not a work of visual art, freezing a moment in time, but more an artistic performance, affecting its audience over an extended period, demands that we bring a different set of questions to the interpretation of this document. They are questions not merely of the inert "given"—of the words inscribed on the page. They are also questions of process and development, of how the reader-text dialogue proceeds over time.

Stanley Fish articulates what strike me as the most fundamental such questions: How is the reader likely to respond to "patterns of expectation and disappointment, reversals of direction, traps, invitations to premature conclusions, textual gaps, delayed revelations, [and] temptations, all of which are related to a corresponding set of authors' intentions? . . ."[21] Though Fish is here seeking to define the general enterprise of reader-response criticism, I can think of no questions more relevant to a reading of the Talmud in particular. Yet, even if the specific questions may change from place to place, the overarching questions remain the same: How does the rhetorical formulation of the literature—in this case, the Talmud—affect the reader's response? How does it shape the message that he hears?

These are, I would argue, more than mere academic questions; they have significant consequences for our understanding of the Talmud's communication. Only through a method of reading such as the one just described will we begin to recover meanings that reside in the

Talmud's extended message (the sugya). And these meanings, I would suggest, are the uniquely *Talmudic* meanings—those that transcend the individual teachings which have so often been the focus of critics' attentions in the past. We shall see in subsequent chapters that these new readings raise new possibilities—the possibility that the Talmud bears meanings and ideologies which have earlier been neglected, if appreciated at all. These readings will challenge contemporary scholars to think about late antique rabbinism in new ways, and to reframe conceptions of the rabbis' piety and purpose. To the extent that my specific readings convince, these new visions of rabbinic religion will contribute to a revision of prior scholarly characterizations. But reading is always, in part, subjective, and different readers of the Bavli will therefore disagree on particular meanings. I invite dispute, and hope that the method illustrated, more than the meanings claimed, contributes to new directions and possibilities in our readings of the rabbis.

The texts I have chosen to read are texts which have beckoned my attention in the past—some because of the centrality of their concerns to classical rabbinism and some because of the centrality of their concerns to contemporary scholarship. In chapter 2, I begin by reading the Bavli's most extended deliberation on the relationship between the Written and Oral Torahs. Rabbinic Judaism is, in Neusner's language, "the Judaism of the Dual Torah." One cannot begin to make sense of rabbinic religion before one grasps the relationship of these two Torahs in the view of any particular stage of the development of that religion. The sugya examined here constitutes the Bavli's most explicit statement on this matter. In chapter 3, I analyze a text which addresses the relationship of Written and Oral Torah more indirectly. The sugya discusses the earlier rabbinic claim that when the Written Torah requires "an eye for an eye," it actually means monetary compensation. This sugya, apparently seeking to show the congruence between the Torah's record and the tradition of the Oral Torah, actually highlights the difficulty of demonstrating such a congruence. The reader comes away feeling that the "fit" of the two Torahs is far from perfect. Having discovered the talmudic recognition of the possibility of misfit, I then turn in chapter 4 to the Talmud's deliberation on the one Mishnah (Ḥagigah, chap. 1, end) that states this possibility outright. This sugya records the Talmud's struggle with what I call "tradition and innovation in rabbinic law," a struggle in which the claim for the traditionality of Oral Torah is finally undermined by the admission of innovation. If I am correct in this reading, the Talmud signals to its reader that, despite apologetic claims to the contrary, the rabbinic system is in significant measure the construction of the rabbis themselves.

In chapters 5 and 6 I turn in a related and equally crucial direction. Perhaps because of the rabbis' recognition of the human component of their Judaism of the Oral Torah, the rabbinic system came to be characterized by its theoretical and practical pluralism. Particular interpretations could always be joined by others. Practices based upon such interpretations, even when differing with practices of neighboring communities, found support. In chapter 5, I explore a sugya that probes the value of theoretical pluralism; in chapter 6 I consider one which asks about the practical consequences of such pluralism. In both cases the Talmud indicates (in my reading) that both theoretical and practical pluralism are not merely supported but are even valued. The Judaism of the Dual Torah is, we discover, also the Judaism of the Alternative Opinion and the Judaism of the Multiplicity of Practices.

Classical Rabbinic Judaism was also, beginning with the Mishnah that provided its foundation, a Judaism of lists and categories. One of its primary concerns was to define category limits and to assign each of the world's components to its appropriate category. Such category definitions distinguished all levels of reality, from large to small. What is proper, what not proper? Who is obligated, who not? These categories commented on the nature and quality of their members. If you knew to which category you belonged, you knew who you were. In chapter 7 I read two sugyot which work on the category "women": In which categories do they belong and why? Are these category assignments essential or conventional? In chapter 8, I consider the same questions as they pertain to Jewish men, in which the concern is both what defines "Jewish" (as opposed to non-Jewish) and what defines "men." The talmudic sugya at hand purportedly focuses on the foreskin and its technical consequences, but as my reading progresses I begin to discern unexpected inflections of the sign "foreskin"—foreskin as a sign of the "other," of he who is impure, non-Jew, nonmale, nonlife.

In chapter 9 I read the Bavli's longest deliberation on the problem of human suffering. This discussion is in substance unrelated to earlier discussions; my interest in this sugya originated with my research into rabbinic views on suffering (see my *Responses to Suffering in Classical Rabbinic Literature*). But the present reading illustrates once again methods employed earlier, and this sugya is particularly rich for the way it utilizes a variety of rhetorical maneuvers to undermine the confident theologies with which it begins. Compiling the canonical range of opinions and then challenging each opinion in turn, this sugya shows (in my reading) the critical nature of the Bavli at its finest, as well as its committed support of what we might call "unorthodox" alternatives.

In chapter 10, I compare the method illustrated here with other methods of reading the Bavli. I seek to show how the approach I propose does greater justice to the Bavli and its possibilities than other contemporary and traditional approaches. But, of course, by that point you will already have read this book and, as always, you will judge for yourself.

2.

Torah,
Written and Oral

The talmudic sugya communicates by means of detailed argumentation, in which details provide the bricks and give-and-take the mortar of the final talmudic structure. The meaning of the communication depends upon both the nature of the bricks and how they are assembled, and it is essential to attend to both before any claims about the Talmud's meaning may be made. What sorts of "bricks" are chosen? Do they repeat? Do they have the same function in different contexts? And so forth. These are all questions which the reader/student must ask. Moreover, as I suggested in the preceding chapter, the Talmud demands that the reader provide some of the "mortar" himself. He must therefore also ask where gaps are left in the Talmud's "masonry" and what the significance of these gaps may be. Always—we, as readers, insist—there will be a meaning in this construction. What it is will depend upon the unique formulation of a given sugya and the response this formulation evokes in the reader/student.

To begin illustrating the consequences of reading the Talmud as literature, I consider a text that elaborates the Bavli's views concerning Written and Oral Torah. Though the Bavli widely assumes these categories, it does not often speak of them.[1] Yet they are fundamental to any discussion of what is unique to rabbinic Judaism. Because of the centrality of these concepts to rabbinic religion, I select for examination in this chapter the Bavli's longest discussion of Written and Oral

Torah and their relation (Git. 60a–b). The text shows signs of careful,
deliberate formulation and, in the opinion of this reader, the hand of
the author reveals a notable artistic sense. To appreciate the sugya's
rhetoric, we require extensive portions of the text at hand. To prevent
the analysis from becoming unwieldy, I divide the talmudic deliberation into smaller units, but full understanding demands that we, finally, view the text as a unified whole.

The deliberation that concerns us is located in its present place by
virtue of a technical association: In its discussion relevant to the Mishnah, the gemara quotes a question sent by "the children of the Galil
to R. Ḥelbo"; the present discussion of Torah, its shape and limits,
also begins with a question directed to R. Ḥelbo by members of the
same community. The sugya's opening section is this:

a. The children of the Galil sent to R. Ḥelbo: What is it to read
   in ḥumashim [scrolls containing only one of the five books of
   the Torah] in public in the synagogue? [Is it permissible or
   not?]

b. He did not know the answer.

c. He came and asked it of R. Isaac Napḥa.

d. He did not know the answer.

e. He came and asked in the study hall, and they derived it from
   that which R. Samuel b. Naḥmani said R. Yoḥanan said:

f. A Torah scroll which is lacking one column, one may not read
   from it [suggesting that one similarly may not read from a scroll
   containing only one book of the Torah, which is missing many
   columns from the complete Torah].

g. But it is not so [that this conclusion follows from the quoted
   opinion]; there [in the case cited by R. Samuel b. Naḥmani in
   the name of R. Yoḥanan] there is something missing, [but]
   here [in the case of the ḥumash] nothing is missing [because
   you are at least reading from a complete book].

h. Rabbah and R. Yosef both said: We do not read in ḥumashim
   in the synagogue on account of the honor of the congregation
   [they evidently assume that reading such a scroll, as opposed to
   a complete Torah, would be contrary to the congregation's
   honor].

i. And Rabbah and R. Yosef both said: This book of haftarot [se-
   lected portions from the prophetic books that are recited ritually

    following the Torah-reading on Shabbat morning and other special occasions], it is prohibited to read from it on Shabbat.[2]

   j. What is the reason?

   k. Because it is not permitted to be written [in the first place, since it contains only smaller sections of larger biblical books].

   l. Mar b. R. Ashi said: To handle it is also prohibited.

   m. What is the reason?

   n. Because it is not fit to read from [for reasons stated above in k.].

   o. But it is not so! It is permissible to handle it and it is permissible to read from it,[3]

   p. for R. Yoḥanan and R. Shimeon b. Laqish would consult a book of Aggadah [narrative midrash] on Shabbat.

   q. But [being Oral Torah], it is not permitted to be written!

   r. Rather, since it is not possible [to do otherwise for, if it were not written, it would be forgotten], "it is time to act for the Lord—annul Your Torah!" (Ps. 119:126, translated for the present context.)

   s. So, too, here, since it is not possible [to do without books of haftarot, complete scrolls of all the necessary prophets being far too expensive], "it is time to act for the Lord—annul Your Torah!"

If I may rephrase the gemara's initial concern in my own words, the sugya begins by asking whether the canonical limits of individual scriptural books or units (such as the Pentateuch) are, for ritual purposes, inviolable. The Talmud articulates two questions, the first regarding the permissibility of reading scrolls of individual books of the Torah in the synagogue and the second regarding the permissibility of reading scrolls containing the liturgical portions from the prophets (haftarot). In both instances, the larger concern is the problem of writing or reading portions of scripture that are smaller than some canonical whole; scrolls of individual books are smaller than the whole Torah of Moses (which contains five books) and the liturgical prophetic portions are, with a couple of exceptions,[4] all smaller than canonical prophetic books. In the first case, reading sections that are less than some canon is prohibited, but, in the second, ingenious argumentation leads to a positive ruling. The Talmud's reasoning is this: Though ideally books of haftarot should be prohibited, we see elsewhere that R. Yoḥanan and R. Shimeon b. Laqish would refer to a book of aggada (narrative midrash) on the Sabbath despite the fact that, being Oral Torah (a designation not yet used here), its writing should have been proscribed. How could these authorities have justified their actions? Since it was *impossible to do otherwise*—because, in the absence of a written record, this element of the Oral Torah would have been forgotten—it was judged that a relatively minor infringement of the ideal is justified. So too, then, is the infringement of the ideal justified in the case of liturgical prophetic portions (if we required whole books, rather than smaller liturgical portions, many communities would not be able to afford this ritual). Consequently, the canonical boundaries cannot here be respected. As we shall see, both this reasoning and the specific reference to the book of aggada will find meaningful echo below.

The same concern for writing sections of scripture that are less than their canonical whole dominates the next part of the discussion as well.

t. Abbaye asked Rabbah: Is it permissible to write a scroll [containing less than a full book of the Torah] for a child to be instructed with?

u. Ask [this question] of the one who said the Torah was given in scrolls [and] ask [this question] of the one who said the Torah was given sealed.

v. Ask the one who said the Torah was given in scrolls: Since it was [originally] written in scrolls it may [now] be written [in scrolls], or since it was [finally] joined, it is joined [and should not resume its scroll-by-scroll status]?

w. Ask the one who said the Torah was given sealed: Since it was given sealed, we do not write it [in individual scrolls] or perhaps *since it is impossible* [not to write smaller scrolls, because without them it will be impossible to educate children] we may write?

x. He said to him: We do not write [scrolls of smaller scriptural portions].

y. And for what reason?

z. Because we do not write. [emphasis added]

The immediate question here is whether it is permissible to write scrolls of small portions of the Torah to use in the instruction of children. The Talmud tells us that there are two opinions regarding the original giving of the Torah that might predispose one to analyze this question in a certain manner; still, it suggests, the question is open according to both opinions. If one begins with the opinion that the Torah was originally given in smaller, individual scrolls, then one is more likely to answer the present question in the affirmative. Nevertheless, one could still conclude that, since the Torah was finally combined to form the single Torah of Moses, it should remain combined and not be disassembled into its smaller segments. On the other hand, if one begins with the opinion that the Torah was originally given "sealed," then one is more likely to answer the present question by suggesting that it remain sealed. Nevertheless, recognizing that prohibiting the writing of such scrolls might make it impossible to teach children, one might disregard the "ideal" law and permit the writing of smaller portions of the Torah.

This is not an innocent, even-handed analysis of the question and its possible answers. As I said, if one begins with the presumption that the Torah was originally given in smaller scrolls, then one is more likely to answer the present question in the affirmative ("yes, we are permitted to write less than the whole Torah scroll in order to instruct children"). But even if one begins with the "sealed" opinion, one is still more likely to answer this question affirmatively because it may reasonably be analyzed as a case where the principle "since it is impossible [to do otherwise]" applies. The text above already identified two matters that should properly have been prohibited, but because it would have been unrealistic, because self-destructive, to maintain such prohibitions, the law turned out to be permissive. So too we are here now predisposed to think the law should be permissive. According to both analyses, therefore, we should expect an affirmative answer.

That is precisely why the negative answer, given at x, is so surprising. Just as surprising is the manner in which that answer is justified. Avoiding any recourse to logical or source-based justification, the Talmud simply asserts that such scrolls may not be written because they may not be written ("because I said so!"). Such a response might be thought weak, lacking, as it does, any outside source or justification. But, in fact, this is the strongest manner such an answer may be asserted, because there is no room left for challenge.[5] There is no logic to which to offer an alternative and no source to interpret differently.

Indeed, there is good reason to believe that the Bavli is aware that this is the consequence of its present rhetorical posture. At Avodah Zarah 35a, the Bavli quotes a tradition, in the name of Ulla, which declares that "When they issue a decree in the West [Palestine] they do not reveal its reason for a full year lest there be a person who doesn't agree and comes to disregard it." In other words, providing a reason invites evaluation of said reason and opens room for disagreement and dissent. In contrast, issuing a decree without reason means that the decree rests solely upon the authority of the issuer; if that authority is recognized, then those addressed by the decree have no opportunity (or reason) to question what has been demanded of them. Applying this analysis to the text at hand, we must say that the Bavli, at z, wishes to leave no room for question or dissent. If we knew nothing else, we would assume that this is where the law stands: we are not permitted to write scrolls of smaller scriptural portions because Rabbah (presumably) said so. Enough said.

Yet, the text confounds our expectations and proceeds immediately, in what follows, to offer objections:

aa. He objected to him [quoting Mishnah Yoma 3:10]: She [Helene, the queen] made a golden tablet upon which was written the [Torah] portion [pertaining to] the suspected woman [see Numbers, chap. 5. This obviously contained far less than the entire Torah!].

bb. R. Shimeon b. Laqish said in the name of R. Yannai: [It was only written] in "aleph-bet" [just the first letter of each word; this was therefore not a case of someone writing a small section of the Torah with permission].

cc. He objected to him [citing a related baraita]: When he [the officiating priest] writes, he looks at the tablet and writes [on the ritual scroll; see v. 23] what is written on the tablet [suggesting that the tablet contains more than merely the first letter of each word of the curse].

dd. I will say [that the baraita means to say] "*as* is written on the tablet" [but not exactly what is written there].

ee. He objected to him [citing another related baraita]: When he writes, he looks at the tablet and writes what is written on the tablet. What is written on the tablet? "If he laid . . . if he did not lay . . ." [see Num. 5:19–20; this text clearly suggests that more than first letters were written].

ff. What are we dealing with here [in the just cited text]? [With a case where the words were written] with interruption [meaning that whole words, but not the whole text, were written].

gg. [This matter is] a tannaitic dispute:

hh. We may not write a scroll for a child to be instructed with, but if it is his [the scribe's] intention to complete [the scroll] it is permitted. R. Judah says: In [the book of] Genesis [it is permitted so long as one writes] up to the generation of the flood; in Leviticus [it is permitted so long as one writes] up to "and it happened on the eighth day . . ." (Lev. 9:1).

Though Jewish tradition had long before the Bavli defined the boundaries of its canonical books, the desire to defend the defined boundaries against dissolution—represented in Rabbah's negative ruling at x—will not be respected. The objections raised, as just quoted, are striking. Taken from a Mishnah and two related, purportedly contemporaneous traditions, the objections all refer explicitly to a case in which a small portion of Torah text was written and early authorities approved of this fact. Though the opinion prohibiting such writing is defended in each instance, on balance it is clear that the interpretations required for such defenses are forced. Are we really to believe that the second baraita (cc) intends to say "as is written," meaning according to the guidance of what is written (=the first letter of each word!)? Is it reasonable to read the final baraita (ee) as suggesting that only words, but not the whole relevant text, were written on the tablet (as proposed in ff)? Granted, the negative ruling is formally salvaged, but we are unable to escape the impression that the counterevidence brought in the objections is considerably more impressive. Furthermore, to make sure that we are not tempted to accept the negative ruling as conclusive, the Talmud concludes this immediate deliberation by revealing that this question remains a subject of (unresolved) tannaitic debate (in hh).

The meaning of this latter step and its effect in context require elaboration. Under ordinary circumstances, the technical term translated in gg as "[This matter is] a tannaitic dispute" (*ketannai*) serves one of two functions: (1) When there is a dispute between sages of the period of the gemara (amoraim), it may point out that the same dispute is evidenced between mishnaic sages (tannaim). (2) When an objection has been rendered against an amora based on tannaitic authority, the gemara may support the amora by suggesting that there is a tannaitic dispute in the same matter and then quoting the text that supports (at least in part) the amora.

In this case, though, the term performs neither of its ordinary functions. Since we have no amoraic dispute concerning the question at hand (no amora has stated that writing such scrolls *is* permitted!), it is impossible to correlate any such dispute with a tannaitic precedent. Similarly, there is no amoraic opinion here that requires tannaitic defense. The several objections to Rabba's opinion have all been answered and there is no reason to seek additional defense—certainly not if the texts quoted in objection really pose no problem according to the suggested reinterpretations.

Furthermore, not only is this introductory phrase awkward but so, too, is the placement of the baraita quoted here. The language of the baraita is virtually identical with the language of the precipitating question (t). It responds directly to that same question, offering two opinions concerning the correct ruling. We might have expected, therefore, that this text be quoted first, not last—particularly since it does not, in context, perform the task its introduction would lead us to anticipate. So what *is* the purpose of quoting this text here, and why introduce it with a term that is, at best, not fully appropriate?

These questions may both be tentatively answered by noting the gemara's evident tendency to avoid closure in this matter. Denying closure of the deliberation itself, the gemara refuses to close off the range of permissible copies of scripture at the defined limits of canonical books. The tannaitic dispute introduced here, at the end of the gemara's treatment of this specific issue, reopens a deliberation that had successfully concluded. It reopens the possibility of granting permission when the gemara would seem already to have rendered its verdict for prohibition. With the inclusion of this dispute, we have tannaitic authority for both rulings, and neither, in the end, is preferred. It seems to me that this is the purpose of leaving this text to last: the gemara, as I understand it, *wants* to leave us with a lack of closure. In fact, up to this point, the gemara has all along preferred to fight against closure, allowing instead the dissolution of canonical limits or boundaries. As we proceed, we shall see whether this preference is upheld.

The next section of this deliberation, returning to the question of how the Torah was originally revealed, persists in confounding the boundaries of scripture that we have come to know.

ii. R. Yoḥanan said in the name of R. Banaʾah: The Torah was given in scrolls, as it is said "Then I said, behold, I have come with the scroll of the book that is written for me" (Ps. 40:8).

jj. R. Shimeon b. Laqish says: The Torah was given sealed, as it is said "[And it happened, when Moses completed writing the words of this Torah in a book, until they were finished, that Moses commanded the Levites . . . saying,] Take this Torah book . . ." (Deut. 31:24–26).

There is little here to suggest an interpretation of these opinions, but the scriptural prooftexts, at least, offer a direction. The text employed by R. Shimeon is taken from a context in which it is unambiguous that Moses completed the writing of the Torah only at the end of the forty-year sojourn in the desert. This leads the well-known rabbinic commentator Rashi (1040–1105) to interpret the term "sealed" in this way:

It [the Torah] was not written until the end of the forty years, until all of the portions were revealed, and those that were revealed to him [= Moses] in the first years were recalled by memory until [at the end of the forty years] he wrote them.

Other commentators dispute details, but they agree that the Torah was revealed—even according to the "sealed" opinion—piece by piece over the course of forty years. The same must be true, therefore, of the "scrolls" position, and the only difference between them, then, is whether each section of Torah was written by Moses as it was revealed or whether some sections, at least, were preserved orally, by memory, until they were finally written down.

The impact of these opinions is crucial. Why, in a larger tradition that speaks of the whole Torah as having preexisted creation (see b. Pes. 54a and b. Ned. 39b), would the notion that the whole Torah was revealed in one event at Mount Sinai not at least be considered here? And why would one of the opinions insist that the Written Torah was originally, at least in part, preserved *orally?* Why discompose the "sealed" whole and flirt with the possibility that it was, during the forty years in the desert in any case, in no essential way different from the Oral Torah (which, as the contemporary myth would have it, was also revealed at that time)?

After a brief elaboration (not reproduced here) of the opinions quoted most recently, the Talmud begins to make clear the meaning of these factors in the context of its larger concern. The deliberation continues:

kk. . . .

ll. R. Eleazer said: The Torah, most of it is in writing and the smaller portion [of it] is oral, as it is said "Though I write for him greater parts of my Torah, they are reckoned as strange" (Hos. 8:12, translated for the present context).

mm. R. Yoḥanan said: Most is oral and less is in writing, as it is said "for by word of these things . . ." (Exod. 34:27, translated for the present context).

Here, for the first time in this text, "Torah" means something other than the five books of Moses. With no forewarning, "Torah" suddenly encompasses other teachings and traditions, apparently what is known by the rabbis at this stage of development as the Oral Torah. The debate is not whether such a Torah was indeed revealed to Moses at Sinai—that is apparently taken for granted—but which of the Torahs, Oral or Written, is larger.

There is reason to doubt, however, whether this is, in fact, the precise question. Rashi interprets the phrase "in writing" in this way: "Most of the Torah is dependent on midrash, for [the Written Torah] is written to be interpreted by means of . . . the rules of Torah interpretation." For Rashi, the Torah "in writing" means not the Written Torah but the Written Torah and all that is derived from it, that is, much of what is commonly called by the rabbis "Oral Torah." What forces Rashi into such a position? The answer, I believe, is the obvious absurdity of Eleazer's claim that most of the Torah is in writing. It must certainly be evident to Eleazer, as it is to us, that most of rabbinic Torah is included not in the Written Torah document but in the extensive rabbinic traditions that define Jewish practice. The Yerushalmi, long before Rashi, understands that this must be so, and in its version Eleazer himself challenges the possibility that most of the Torah is written, suggesting instead that "more numerous are those things that are derived from the Written than those derived from the Oral" (y. Pe' a 2:4, 17a and y. Ḥag. 1:8, 76d). According to both the Yeru-

shalmi and Rashi, therefore, the dispute is one of ultimate source: Is
the majority of the law in some way connected to the Written Torah,
or was it revealed to Moses independently, without any direct connection to the Written Torah?

If this interpretation is correct—and we, knowing the absurdity of
Eleazar's opinion understood literally, will tend to believe it is—then
the "Torah in writing" here means not the Written Torah, but that
part of Oral Torah that is called "written" by virtue of its derivation
from the Written Torah. In this usage, any distinction between what
are conventionally known as Written and Oral Torah is rhetorically
eliminated and, though we may debate the sources of law, various
laws with these different sources ultimately blend into a single contin-
uum of divine authority.

The sense that the conventional categories finally disintegrate is
similarly evident in the discussion that follows:

nn.   . . .

oo.   R. Judah b. Naḥmani, the spokesperson of R. Shimeon b.
      Laqish expounded: It is written "write for yourself these things"
      (Exod. 34:27) and it is written "for by word of these things"
      (ibid.). How can these be reconciled? Things that are written
      [Written Torah] you are not permitted to say them orally [and]
      things that are Oral you are not permitted to state in writing.

pp.   It is taught in the school of R. Ishmael: "[Write for yourself]
      these" (Exod. 34:27)—these you may write but you may not
      write laws [legal traditions of the Oral Torah].

qq.   R. Yohanan said: The Holy One, blessed be He, established
      His covenant with Israel only on account of things that are
      oral, for it is said "for by word of these things did I establish
      with you a covenant, and with Israel" (ibid.).

Here, ironically, Written and Oral Torah are for the first time definitively distinguished: what is Oral may not be written and what is
Written may not be kept orally. But, upon closer inspection, it becomes clear that this distinction is illusory, for the text provides evidence that the stated prohibition is not heeded and the distinction it
protects therefore not respected. To begin with, we learned at the beginning of this long deliberation that the prohibition enunciated here
has been disregarded by R. Yohanan and R. Shimeon b. Laqish, who,
it will be recalled, referred to a book of aggada (written Oral Torah).

Moreover, the prohibition itself is the opinion of one "R. Judah b. Naḥmani the spokesperson of R. Shimeon b. Laqish." Ordinarily, such a spokesperson would be expected simply to repeat the exact words of his master. At the very least, we can be sure that the opinion of a spokesperson circulated in the school of his master and most likely had his approval. And yet it is the very master of this spokesperson, R. Shimeon b. Laqish, who is described as being one of the two people who disregards this prohibition. If this prohibition was ever heeded, in other words, its power was lost in what is, historically speaking, a mere instant. Though in theory Oral should remain oral and Written, written, in fact, Oral was quickly written down, and this distinction, like others in theory, did not last.

The reason for all this becomes clear in the end. The covenant with Israel, we discover (at qq), was established primarily because of the Oral Torah. The centrality of Oral Torah is articulated here clearly and without compromise, and there can be little doubt that it was toward this end that the Talmud was leading all along.

By refusing to respect the immutable boundaries of canonical books—smaller scrolls, defined by the scribe or the liturgical community, *may* be written—the Bavli challenged also the conceptual integrity of these boundaries. By allowing scripture to be recorded in smaller and smaller pieces, the Bavli caused scripture ultimately to approach disintegration. Large texts became small and small texts became mere words; words, of course, are the stuff of Oral Torah. At the same time, we learned, Written Torah was originally, at most, smaller scrolls—again, approaching units of speech—and, according to one of two opinions, Written Torah was originally oral. In effect, the only difference between Written and Oral Torah during the life of Moses was what they would one day become; for most of that period, the form of the two Torahs was literally identical.

Similarly, the Oral Torah is also written, on two accounts. First, that part of Oral Torah that is derived from the Written is called written in this text. Second, the Oral Torah is literally written because "it is impossible" to do otherwise; to ensure its preservation, it must be written. Just as the Written Torah was once oral, so too is the Oral Torah now written. Boundaries disintegrate. The categories merge.

We see here in the Bavli that the Oral Torah is canonized as Sinaitic revelation in the fullest sense. At the earliest stages of the development of Rabbinic Judaism, this could by no means be taken for granted. In rabbinic documents produced as late as the early fourth century, there is a pronounced ambivalence toward the comparative status of the rabbinic, "Oral" Torah. But here, at the latest stage of the development of classical rabbinism, that ambivalence has been overcome. Oral Torah is Torah, in the fullest sense of the term. And whatever distinction might once have been maintained between one form of Torah and the other now effectively disappears. After all, it was all part of the original divine revelation, and thus there can be no reason to distinguish the fundamental authority of one from that of the other. Understood this way, this text shows, more than any other, the wisdom of Jacob Neusner's claim that there is in rabbinic Judaism no canon other than the whole Torah.[6]

Would we have realized this conclusion if we had approached this gemara with a different lens? In part, perhaps, but without the same thoroughness of conviction. On the halakhic level, the questions are whether we are permitted to write smaller scrolls or to read written Oral Torah. These and similar questions may certainly be answered based upon this text, but by employing such a lens, we allow the text to fall apart. To answer these questions, one at a time, we need only small sections of the overall sugya. We need not ask what the total orchestration accomplishes. The alternative perspective, modelled here, seeks more subtle meanings, communicated through formulation and symbolic association. It may fairly be said that the author(s) didn't necessarily appreciate—with full consciousness, that is—all of the meanings we have discovered. Are the meanings there, then, in the text as it is written? If we may discover these meanings and defend them with reference to the text as composed, then they are there. If our "Oral Torah"—our interpretation—makes intimate connections with the Talmud's written Torah, then they are one.

3.

The Rabbis
and Scripture

In the last chapter, we examined the Bavli's most detailed discussion of the relationship of the Written and Oral Torahs, understanding the sugya as asserting the fundamental equality of these two forms. But for those familiar with the Bavli's method of exposition, this conclusion may not rest easily, for they will surely know that the Bavli, like other rabbinic documents before it (excluding the Mishnah and the Tosefta), constantly refers to Written Torah for support of rabbinic opinions. Why else, if not the recognized superior authority of Written Torah, would this exercise be so ubiquitous?

Modern critics might respond that the practice of justifying rabbinic opinions by reference to the Written Torah is merely a rhetorical apologetic that supports the authority of rabbinic law on the basis of the recognized authority of Written law. In fact, they will go on to argue, the *real* authority lies in the hands of the rabbis, who interpret the Written Torah to support their own Torah. In rabbinic midrash, the Written Torah means what the rabbis say it means. If the rabbis choose to dismiss the simple meaning of a scriptural verse, there is no authority who can veto their choice. Thus, this argument will conclude, whatever the purpose of the rhetoric, the rabbis' Oral Torah is indeed equal to the Written in authority, if not superior.

Whatever the merit of this analysis, the more crucial question is not the relative authority and relationship of the two Torahs in reality, but their relationship as understood by the rabbis—for our purposes, the authors of the Bavli. Did these rabbis really mean to propose an equation of Written and Oral Torah, as suggested in the preceding chapter, or does their common "proof-texting" by reference to Written Torah show their respect of its superior and final authority? When they refer to scriptural prooftexts, is this a mere formality—a rhetorical exercise—or do they believe that the support of Written Torah is necessary before a rabbinic opinion can be deemed fully authoritative? Perhaps most fundamentally, do they understand the consequence of their interpretive practices? Do they understand, and are they willing to admit, that the final authority in reality resides with them? These are the questions a full accounting of the rabbis' relationship with scripture must answer. These are the questions for which we will begin to seek answers in this chapter.

One text that reflects upon these questions, indirectly but at great length, is the sugya at Baba Qamma 83b–84a which asks whether injury to another person requires monetary compensation or literal "eye-for-eye" payment. What makes the sugya particularly interesting is that the Mishnah requires the former, though the Torah seems clearly to support the latter. This tension requires that the simple meanings of the Mishnah and Torah be reconciled, an exercise that relates directly to our questions concerning the relationship of these two bodies of law. Predictably, the gemara asserts in the end that the Mishnah's law (monetary compensation) is what the Torah really intended all along. What is less expected is the way the gemara goes about this; its deliberation, I will argue, communicates discontinuity in spite of its final formal support of the contrary.

This is a sugya that compiles a number of midrashim from various talmudic periods, all of which relate to the question at hand: Is the Torah's "eye for eye" to be taken literally or not? Two factors are constantly at play: (1) the level of authority of the cited midrash (some are tannaitic, some amoraic), and (2) the success or failure of any given proof (some succeed and some fail). Also demanding attention is the logic of each proposed proof, successful or failed, and the degree to which its reading seems to reflect the simple or most natural meaning of scripture. As we consider the play of these factors, we will find that this is a sugya whose deliberative posture belies its stated goal.

The text is composed of a total of ten approaches to the central question, the first of which follows.

Mishnah: One who injures his neighbor is liable for five sorts [of restitution] . . .

Gemara
I.

   a. Why [is payment required]? The Merciful One said [in scripture], "eye for eye!" (Exod. 21:24) Let me say literally an eye!

   b. You should not think this, for it is taught: Is it possible that, if he blinded his eye, he should blind his eye [in return]? If he cut off his hand, he should cut off his hand? If he broke his leg, he should break his leg? Scripture says "One who smites a human" and "one who smites a beast" (Lev. 24:21?; see c through e below)—just as the one who smites a beast makes payment, so, too, does one who smites a human make payment. And if you wish to say [as an alternative proof], behold, He says, "You may not accept ransom for the life of a murderer [who is guilty of a capital crime]¹" (Num. 35:31)—for the life of a murderer you may not take ransom, but you do take ransom [payment] [even] for limbs that do not heal.

   c. Which "smite" [is intended in the first part of this midrash, in b]?

   d. If you say, "One who smites a beast shall make restitution for it; but one who smites a human shall be put to death" (Lev. 24:21), that [verse] is written concerning [cases of] murder [and so should not be used to teach the law for mere injury]!

   e. Rather, from here: "One who smites a beast shall make restitution for it, life for life," (ibid., v. 18) and juxtaposed to it² [we read], "If anyone maims his fellow, as he has done so shall it be done to him" (v. 19).

   f. [But] this [v. 19] is not [a case where scripture says] "smite"!

   g. We mean to say "smiting" [should be equated with] "smiting" [though there is no actual equation of scriptural terms used]. Just as the smiting that is spoken of with regard to the beast [requires] payment, so, too, [with] the smiting that is spoken of with regard to humans, there is payment . . .³

   h. And what is [the need for] "And if you wish to say" [in the midrash at b above]?

   i. Moreover, it is a problem for the tanna: What have you seen that causes you to learn from the smiting of a beast? Learn [the law, instead,] from the smiting of a person!

j. They say [in response to this problem]: We derive [laws of] damages from damages and we do not derive damages from killing.

k. On the contrary! We [should] derive [laws regarding] a person from [laws regarding] a person and we [should] not derive [laws regarding] a person from [laws regarding] a beast!

l. [You are correct, and] this is why it teaches "And if you wish to say," thus, He says, "You may not accept ransom for the life of a murderer who is guilty of a capital crime" (Num. 35:31)— for the life of a murderer you may not take ransom, but you do take ransom [payment] [even] for limbs that do not heal.

m. This [verse] "You may not accept ransom for the life of a murderer," does it come to exclude limbs [from the lex talionis]? But it is required for the Merciful One to say, "Don't do two things to him; don't take payment from him *and* put him to death!"

n. This [law] is derived from [the scripture] "as his guilt warrants!" (Deut. 25:2)—You hold him liable for one guilt but you do not hold him liable for two guilts [for the same act]!

o. But it [the verse first mentioned in the second part of b and now questioned in m] is still required for the Merciful One to say, "Don't take payment [from him, in a case of murder] and release him!"

p. If so [that is, if this is all it may be used to teach], the Merciful One should have written "You may not accept ransom for the one who is guilty of a capital crime"; why do I need "for the life of a murderer"? [Obviously it would be a murderer who is "guilty of a capital crime"!] [Therefore, we may] learn from this [extraneous phrase that] for the life of a murderer you may not take ransom, but you do take ransom [payment] [even] for limbs that do not heal.

q. But, since it is written "You may not accept ransom" [which, we have just established, may be used to learn that payment is required for injury and not retribution in kind], why do I need [the first derivation, equating] "smite" [with] "smite"?

r. They say [in response], if [only] from this [second derivation ("Don't take ransom . . . ")] I might have said [that] if he wants he may give his eye and if he wants he may give the worth of his eye; [therefore, this first derivation] comes to teach us [the law] from a beast; just as the one who smites a beast makes payment, so, too, does one who smites a human make payment.

This first approach, the longest of any in this sugya, is built on analysis of a baraita, b, which offers two proofs for the conclusion that "eye for eye" must be understood to require monetary compensation. The first proof, according to its simple meaning, is from an equation of scriptural terms (*gezeira shava*) and the second from a close, deductive reading of a particular verse (a *diuq*). But the gemara does not accept these proofs passively, and its analysis requires significant revisions in our understanding of the baraita's traditions.

The first problem pointed out by the gemara is that the alleged equation of scriptures has no obvious source (c through d). Not able to identify the verses in which the common word appears, the text suggests that the equation be understood imprecisely (g), claiming that concepts are being equated, but not precise terms. But this revision does not eliminate our problems, for two reasons: First, if the first proof were adequate, why would a second one (h) be needed? Second, what is the logic of equating concepts that appear in two different settings, one speaking of people and one of beasts? Wouldn't it be preferable to equate people with people and beasts with beasts (i and k)? The gemara grants the validity of this latter objection (inviting the reader to do the same) and suggests that it is for this very reason that the second proof is necessary (see l). But this second proof, too, is problematic (m and o) and, though a successful resolution to the problem is found (p), one is left with the clear impression that things are not quite as tidy as they ought to be. In fact, though in the end the proofs suggested in the baraita are upheld (with, however, significant emendation of the first), it may well be difficult for the reader confidently to reproduce the purported source of the proffered conclusion. When all is said and done, what *is* the proof that "eye for eye" must be understood in other than literal fashion?

This impression is strengthened by what follows. Despite the fact that this first proof was salvaged—it is, finally, "successful"—the gemara now goes on to quote and analyze many more proofs. What need could there be for doing so? In a strictly logical system, the strongest proof of any position is a single, successful one. Adding another proof only calls the success of the first demonstration into question. After all, if we have convincingly shown that there is a scriptural source for a particular law, what possible need could there be of another source or proof? This question is particularly sharp in the Talmudic context, in which it is assumed that all scriptures have a purpose and that no scripture, therefore, will ever be redundant. Redundancy is evidence of a problem! Consequently, adding proofs can only be justified if we admit that the first proof is only "one person's" interpretation—neither the only possible proof nor immune to challenge. Only in a system that is not strictly logical (in which "logic" means the self-defined logic of the system)—a system in which there may be preferences but no confidence in a single, indisputable position—can the piling up of proofs be justified. Still, even in such a system, the more proofs adduced, the less convincing will any individual proof appear.

The second proof emphatically highlights the provisional nature of this whole interpretive enterprise.

II.

    a. It is taught: R. Dostai b. Judah says: "Eye for eye"— [this means] money [as restitution]. You say money? Or perhaps it means literally an eye? You say—Lo, if this one's eye was large and this one's eye small, how could I [literally] apply to it "eye for eye?" And should you say [that] in any case like this [one just described] collect money from him [but, where possible, apply the law literally], the Torah said, "You shall have one standard" (Lev. 24:22), [meaning] a law that is equal for all of you [and what you have suggested would not fulfill this requirement. Thus, taking monetary payment from all is the only viable alternative.].

    b. They say: What is the problem? Maybe he took sight from him [and] sight, the Merciful One said, we should take from him!

    c. For, if you do not say this, [84a] [in a case where] a small person killed a big person or a big person killed a small person [in which there is no question, being a capital case, that retribution requires "life for life"], how do we kill him? The Torah said, "You shall have one standard!" Rather, [obviously] he took his life from him, so his life, the Merciful One said, we should take from him.

    d. So too, here, he took sight from him [and] sight, the Merciful One said, we should take from him! [Since this is a reasonable reading of the verse in question, the logic used in (a) is no good and this proof fails.]

In this second case, the Talmud concludes that the proffered proof—a baraita—fails. The proof is based, readers are forced to admit, on a ridiculous reading of the Torah's law (literal retribution means that the eyes must be precisely the same size!), and the gemara (b and d) voices exactly the interpretation that we, the readers, would likely have proposed from the very beginning. We know the that proof asks us to yield too much, and so we, with the gemara's approval, judge against the proposed proof. But we must recognize the implications of doing so.

The rejected proof is, as indicated, a tannaitic tradition, every bit as authoritative as the first proof, which, in the end, the gemara was able to support (though not without misgivings). The present rejection means that we are not bound by the authority of the inherited tradition in all of its parts! It is legitimate to analyze that tradition and, where fitting, to reject it. Moreover, in the present context, the rejection leads to a startling possibility: If this logic is flawed, then there is a good reading of the verses at hand which accepts the viability of a lex talionis. In other words, as far as the present approach is concerned, it may well be correct to read "eye for eye" literally! Certainly, at this immediate juncture in the sugya, that is the more reasonable alternative.

One might suggest that this rejection is intended to demonstrate the correctness and authority of the first proof. By rejecting other proofs, we might think, the first is strengthened. But this gemara has no particular investment in the first proof; several alternative proofs follow, some of which succeed and some of which fail. Moreover, there is no apparent priority of one proof to another. True, straight tannaitic proofs come first, followed by tannaitic proofs "of the school of," and finally by amoraic proofs. But within the categories proofs might succeed or not. There is no hint that one sort of proof is preferred to another, and the overall cacophony of proposals leads to the inescapable impression that the masters of the tradition are willing to go to almost any lengths to "prove" that monetary compensation is what is required. But, as the Talmud demonstrates, many of these masters do protest too much. The vulnerability of the whole enterprise is made apparent to all. Most important, in the end it is impossible to declare which scripture proves what these masters want to prove. For the question "How do we know that the Torah requires monetary compensation?" there simply is no ready answer.

But I have jumped ahead too quickly. Let us examine the next suggested proof—one which indeed learns a lesson from the failure of the preceding proof but nevertheless itself also fails, in the end, to prove that monetary compensation is what the Torah demands.

III.

   a. There is another teaching—

   b. R. Shimeon b. Yoḥai says: "Eye for eye"—[this means] money [as restitution]. You say money? Or perhaps it means literally an eye? You say—Lo, if he was blind and he blinded, an amputee and he amputated, lame and he made [someone] lame, how could I [literally] apply to it "eye for eye" when the Torah said, "You shall have one standard" (Lev. 24:22), [meaning] a law that is equal for all of you [and what you have suggested would not fulfill this requirement. Thus, taking monetary payment from all is the only viable alternative].

   c. They say: What is the problem? Maybe where it is possible it is possible [and we impose the law of "eye for eye" and] where it is not possible it is not possible and we dismiss him [without liability].

   d. For if you do not say this, [in the case of] a [person] afflicted [with a fatal disease] who killed a healthy [person; such a person cannot, for technical reasons, be put to death], what do we do to him?

   e. Rather, when it is possible it is possible and when it is not possible it is not possible and we dismiss him [without liability].

This approach follows the preceding in many of its details. Unlike the preceding, it does not suggest the "ridiculous" possibility that one eye must be exactly like the other. Instead, it accepts that the verse is speaking of sight (="eye"), the ability to walk (="leg"), and the like. Its difficulty with the verse lies in the fact that there are individuals who might injure others in parts of their person that the injurers do not possess. Therefore, the baraita argues (again, the proof is found in a baraita), the verse must intend monetary compensation.

But, again, this proof appears forced—as the gemara (and the reader with it) readily admits. Do laws admit to no exceptions? Do the few exceptions force us to throw laws out entirely? Or is it not more reasonable to understand laws as broad guidelines, guidelines that do, however, admit to exceptions? In other words, when it is possible to apply a law, we should, but when a rare exception presents itself— when it is impossible to apply a law—then we should not do so. What choice do we have?

Any legal system must operate this way, upholding its laws despite occasional difficulties or exceptions. Not surprisingly, the gemara is easily able to point to just such a case in its capital law (d), and so the reading of the law that allows for rare exceptions is shown to be reasonable even within the limits of associated rabbinic law. Indeed, such a conclusion is the necessary and reasonable one in any viable legal system. Consequently, the Torah, when it declares "eye for eye," might readily mean just what it says (though making room for the rare exception). The proof fails. The authority of the tanna carries no weight in the face of compelling contrary reasoning.

Unlike the two proofs just considered, the next two proofs, closely parallel to each other, do succeed. But even these are not without problems, and the problems invite us to second-guess the stated conclusions. Again, it will not be clear that the proposed proofs are above question and that the Torah, therefore, means "money" when it says "eye." The arguments follow.

IV.
  a. It is taught of the school of R. Ishmael: Scripture says, "so shall it be inflicted on him [literally: given in him]" (Lev. 24:20) and "giving" is none other than monetary payment.
  b. But, based on this logic, "As he shall give an injury to a person" (ibid., translated for context) is this also monetary payment?!
  c. They say: [The baraita] "of the school of R. Ishmael" [means to] interpret superfluous scripture—since it is written, "If anyone maims his fellow, as he has done so shall it be done to him" (ibid., v. 19) why do I [also] need "so shall it be inflicted on him?"
  d. Learn from this [superfluousness]: monetary payment.
  e. [But] why do I need "As he shall give an injury in a person?"
  f. Since it [the Torah] wants to write "so shall it be inflicted on him" it also writes "As he shall give an injury in a person" [for stylistic balance].

V.

  a. It is taught of the school of R. Ḥiyya: Scripture says, "hand for hand [literally: hand in hand]," (Deut. 19:21) [meaning] something that is given from hand to hand. And what is it? Money.

  b. But, based on this logic, "foot for foot" (ibid.), is it also [to be understood] like this? [Obviously not!]

  c. They say: [the baraita] "of the school of R. Ḥiyya" [means to] interpret superfluous scripture—since it is written, "You shall do to him as he schemed to do to his fellow" (ibid., v. 19), [and] if you think [that this scripture is to be taken] literally, why do I need "hand for hand?"

  d. [Rather,] learn from this [superfluousness]: monetary payment.

  e. [So] why do I need "foot for foot?"

  f. Since it is written "hand for hand" [God] also wrote "foot for foot."

In both of these cases, a particular scripture is subjected to a close reading and taken to suggest that monetary payment is required. In both cases, the logic of the reading is challenged (b) and the gemara then suggests a revised reading that salvages the desired conclusion. But it must be understood how this is accomplished. In both cases, the proof is said to be based, in the end, upon superfluous scripture. However, it will be evident to all that, in both cases, this claim contradicts the simple meaning of the original proposed proof. In effect, the proofs are deemed faulty and only the verses in question are preserved, to yield, now according to a different reading, the desired conclusion. But even the gemara's own method for arriving at this conclusion is, in both cases, ironically called into question. As stated, the proofs in their revised forms depend on the principle that there is nothing superfluous in scripture. Yet, in the end of each approach (f), it is suggested that certain parts of the central scriptures are needed only to achieve stylistic balance. This is a common explanation, in the gemara, for the formulation of the Mishnah or other tannaitic texts, but it is highly unusual in connection with scripture.[4] Here it only serves to undermine the logic that the gemara uses. There cannot be superfluous scripture, the final answer says, except where there needs to be. The distance that these arguments come from the original proofs cannot be more evident.

Crucially, both of these "successful" proofs make their forced quality immediately apparent. The reader will know that they are formally successful, but he or she will not fail to sense that the success comes at a cost. Earlier authorities are upheld, but only through aggressive rereading by later, anonymous authorities. Furthermore, the reader will notice that, by contrast, those proofs which fail (examined above) require no such rereadings. On the contrary, the logic of the refutations in approaches III and IV could not be simpler or more natural. We are thus forced to ask ourselves, Which outcome makes more sense, the one that upholds the Mishnah's law or the one that maintains the plain meaning of the Torah's words? On its surface, the gemara will want us to accede to the former conclusion, but not before forcing us to admit the wisdom of the latter.

As if to reinforce this impression, the gemara now proceeds by quoting three proofs, none of which, in the end, is upheld. The three approaches follow.

VI.

    a. Abbaye said: [the law] comes from that which is taught of the school of Ḥezkiah, for it is taught of the school of Ḥezkiah—

    b. "eye for eye, soul for soul," and not a soul and an eye for an eye. And if you should think literally [an eye for an eye], there are times when you find an eye and a soul [given] for an eye, for as you blind him his soul [may] go out!

    c. And what is the problem? Perhaps we evaluate him—if he can withstand it [the blinding, without dying] we do it and if he cannot withstand it we do not do it, and if we estimate that he can withstand it and we do it and his breath [nevertheless] leaves him, if he dies, let him die!

    d. Have we not taught with respect to lashes: If they estimated [that he could withstand the lashes] but he died under his hand [the hand of the one administering the lashes] he is exempt [Mishnah Makkot 3:14, with differences]! [By the same token, we make a similar evaluation in this case, and if we are wrong—so be it! The fear of such a mistake should not undermine the literal meaning of "eye for eye."]

VII.

    a. R. Zevid in the name of Rabba said: Scripture said, "wound for wound"—to [require one to] give [payment for] pain in the place [where one also pays for] damages. And if you should think literally [eye for eye], just as this one has pain so too does that one [the one whose eye is now removed in retribution] have pain. [So, being that they would both have pain, what payment would be necessary? Therefore "eye for eye" cannot be taken literally.]

b. And what is the problem? Perhaps there is a person who is sensitive and has greater pain, and a person who is not sensitive [and] he has no pain. And what then derives from it [that is, from the words "wound for wound"]? [The requirement] to give him [the more sensitive party] the difference [payment for his greater pain].

VIII.

a. R. Pappa in the name of Rava said: Scripture said, "He shall be healed"—to [require one to] give [payment for] healing in the place [where one also pays for] damages. And if you should think literally [eye for eye], just as this one requires healing so too does this one require healing [so, being that they would both require healing, what payment would be necessary? Therefore "eye for eye" cannot be taken literally].

b. And what is the problem? Perhaps there is one whose flesh heals quickly and one whose flesh does not heal quickly. And what then derives from it [that is, from the words "he shall be healed]? [The requirement] to give him [the party who heals less quickly] the difference.

Each of these failed proofs follows, more or less, the pattern of the failed proofs seen earlier. In the first instance (VI) an overly literal reading is answered with the suggestion that one ought not be so literal; there will be exceptions and errors will be made. In the latter cases (VII and VIII), related damage payments (for pain and healing) seem to be rendered irrelevant if the punishment is literally an eye for an eye. Therefore, it is suggested, lex talionis cannot be intended. But, recognizing that pain and healing will inevitably be different for different parties, the gemara responds that those payments—and the scriptures that demand them—are not irrelevant, for they are intended precisely to require payment for those inevitable differences.

At this point, the reader cannot help but note that more of the proofs have failed (II, III, VI, VII, and VIII) than have succeeded (I, IV, and V). This imbalance creates a tension: If there were one convincing proof, then why not quote it and leave well enough alone? If the successful proofs are inadequate—perhaps because of the gymnastics necessary to support them—then maybe it is reasonable to consider the wisdom of the failed proofs as well. And if the "failed" proofs, which conclude that "eye for eye" might mean just that, are more numerous and perhaps even less forced, then maybe it is reasonable to conclude that an eye should be taken for an eye. On the basis of the logical merits alone, this conclusion cannot, at this stage of the deliberation, be ruled out.

Two approaches remain in this lengthy sugya, the first formally a successful proof of the claim that "eye for eye" should *not* be taken literally and the second an assertion, to be technically refuted in the end, that "eye for eye" *should* be understood literally. But, we will see, the "successful" proof is saved only with great difficulty, and the refutation of the opinion supporting a literal reading is extremely weak. Despite superficial success in the quest for a proof of the Mishnah's law, it will be difficult not to notice that success has been achieved at a great cost. Crucially, it is the gemara itself that has assured that cost would be known.

First, the "successful" proof.

IX.

    a. R. Ashi said: It comes [by means of an equation of the scriptural terms] "for" [and] "for" from [the use of the same term in connection with an] ox. It is written here "eye *for* eye" and it is written there "he should pay one ox *for* the other" (Exod. 21:36). Just as there [it means] money so too here [it means] money.

    b. What did you see that led you to learn [by means of an equation of the terms] "for" [and] "for" from ox? Learn [instead by means of an equation of the terms] "for" [and] "for" from man, for it is written "and you shall give one soul for another" (Exod. 21:23)—just as there [it means] literally so too here [it means] literally.

    c. They say: We derive damages from damages and we do not derive damages from capital crimes.

    d. On the contrary! We derive [cases involving] persons from [cases involving] persons and we do not derive [cases involving] persons from [cases involving] an animal. [The wisdom of this rejoinder is admitted, so the gemara goes on to suggest:]

e. Rather, R. Ashi learned it from "[and the man who lay with her should give to the father of the girl fifty silver pieces, and she should be his as a wife,] *for* he humbled her" [Deut. 22:29, discussing the case of a girl who has been raped]—[in which case he would be] learning [a case involving] persons from [a case involving] persons and damages from damages.

The present discussion makes it clear that using the term "for" as the foundation for a derivation has its difficulties, not the least of which is the fact that "for" is often used in related contexts, making it difficult to decide which equation is the best. Logically, it makes sense that the law of damage done by one human to another should be derived from another case of damages (not capital liability) involving people (not animals). Therefore, the Talmud proposes (e) that R. Ashi really intended to suggest an equation with Deuteronomy 22:29, in which "for" is found in precisely such a context (damages, human to human).

The problem is that this "solution" contradicts explicitly what R. Ashi is represented as saying at (a). As recorded before us, R. Ashi identifies the verse on the basis of which he wishes to construct the equation. The gemara, in all of its cleverness, may be able to identify a verse that responds to its own logical objections (d), but the verse it proposes simply is *not* the verse cited by (or for) R. Ashi. Moreover, even if we were to suggest that the identification of the verses (in the latter half of a) is the voice of the gemara expanding upon R. Ashi's briefer statement, there is simply no reasonable way for a reader to reduce R. Ashi's teaching to anything less than "It comes 'for' 'for' *from ox*" [emphasis added].[5] Deuteronomy 22:29 does not speak of an ox!

Thus, though R. Ashi's proof is technically salvaged, that saving comes, as we said, at an immense cost—the cost of contradicting, explicitly and undeniably, what R. Ashi is recorded as having said. Has the gemara, in the end, itself come up with a viable proof? Perhaps. But it has gone far afield to do so, and the violence done to the position it is ostensibly supporting weakens any conclusion it might suggest. Does the gemara want to support the law of the Mishnah, ruling that monetary compensation is required in cases of damages? No doubt. Does it want it to appear that that law derives cleanly and easily from a scriptural source? It appears not.

Which brings us to the last part of the sugya. This last approach takes an entirely different direction, deliberating on an opinion which affirms that when the Torah says "eye for eye," it means "eye for eye." This opinion is rejected in the end but, as hinted earlier, this rejection is accomplished with irony, an irony that leads us to question the power of the rejection and ultimate conclusion. The text follows.

X.

    a. It is taught: R. Eliezer says: "Eye for eye"—literally.

    b. Do you [actually] think "literally?!" [But] doesn't R. Eliezer accept all of these tannaim [whose opinions are taught above]?!

    c. Rabbah said: [He merely means] to say that we do not estimate him [his worth] as a slave.

    d. Abbaye said to him: So, like whom? Like a free person?! Does a free person have monetary worth?!

    e. Rather, R. Ashi said: [He means] to say that we do not estimate the worth [to be paid to the injured party] according to the [worth of] the damaged party but according to the [worth of] the damaging party.

Here, we turn back to a tannaitic tradition, one which suggests that scripture's "eye for eye" prescription should be understood literally. In the end, the gemara concludes that R. Eliezer can't really mean this, but it is perfectly clear that this conclusion is forced and unnecessary. The gemara gives us every piece of information we need to reject its own final interpretation.

First, in every prior approach to this question, "literally" (*mamash*) has meant exactly that; it is impossible, at this late stage in the sugya, for the reader to take it any other way. Second, the literal meaning of the term "literally" is rejected here for a reason that the gemara itself has shown to be ridiculous: How could we possibly ask whether R. Eliezer accepts the many tannaitic traditions quoted above when the gemara *itself* has rejected *fully half of them*—and shown the others to be weak in various ways? Furthermore, R. Eliezer is a tanna, and thus has full authority to conclude as he wishes; according to the rules of the game, he is in no way bound by the authority of other tannaim! So, if he wants "literally," he is welcome to "literally"! In addition, the character of R. Eliezer painted throughout rabbinic literature shows him to be a particularly conservative sort, so the interpretation here attributed to him fulfills every expectation that the educated reader has of this master. And, finally, after having studied the various convoluted attempts above to prove that "eye for eye" must mean money—some successful, but a greater number not—the reader will, in all likelihood, respond to R. Eliezer's position with a sigh of relief; "at last," he or she will say, "we have someone who speaks reason." Even if this is too extreme—and I think it is not—R. Eliezer's opinion at least shows that there is another possibility that, even (literally) in the end, merits consideration. The gemara's interpretation denying this conclusion only shows us how urgently the gemara doesn't want us to accept the literal reading in practice. We can support this conclusion but, with the gemara's direction, we will have a hard time accepting that it is the necessary outcome of scripture.

But why, if the gemara supports the Mishnah's law, does it go out of its way to show how difficult it is to prove that law from scripture? The answer, in my understanding, is that the gemara has an interest in demonstrating its ultimate distance from scripture. Its law is related to scripture and often dependent on scripture—but only incompletely so. For the interpretation of the sages—even the later Talmudic sages—is also understood, with great confidence at this late date, to be Torah. Thus, by subjecting earlier scripture-based apologia to this sort of critical analysis, the Talmud declares that the defense of rabbinic law by reference to scripture is not completely necessary. Interpretations are imperfect, alternatives are therefore legitimate, and, when all is said and done, the rabbis may follow their own emotions and reason without submitting absolutely to the apparent dictates of Written Torah. To this reader it seems that, in the present sugya, the rabbinic authors want to demonstrate their fundamental independence from scripture. They want to show that the meaning of scripture—and the desire of its Author—is subject to doubt and that the law will ultimately follow the Oral tradition (in this case, the Mishnah), regardless of the simple meaning of the Written text.

4.

Rhetorics of
Tradition and Innovation

In the preceding chapter, I read Baba Qamma 83b–84a as a statement on the relationship of Written and Oral Torah, of scripture
and rabbinic tradition. In that reading, I understood rabbinic opinions
as bold but muted; remarkably candid, but only by implication. I saw
the larger rhetorical structures—numerous exercises in determining the
purported scriptural source of the Mishnah's law—as undermining the
very goal the gemara had seemingly set out for itself. Constituting, in
my analysis, a major utterance on the priority of rabbinic formulations
vis-à-vis scripture, that sugya offered its testimony only circuitously,
and thus failed to announce the gravity of the question it was ultimately addressing.

The same is not true at Hagigah 10a–11b, in which the Mishnah
demands that the question of the relationship between rabbinic tradition and Torah be confronted directly. The Mishnah observes explicitly that some categories of traditional law have little evident connection with Written Torah. The gemara, therefore, is forced to weigh in
with its own opinion on this subject. Against the potentially troubling
candor of the Mishnah, the gemara appears to respond defensively and
without compromise, insisting that all traditional law has profound
connections with the Written revelation. But, once again, an informed and aggressive reading will show that behind the apologetics
stands another agenda—one that seeks to demonstrate the fundamen-

tal equality of the Written and Rabbinic traditions. Appearances can be deceptive, and what appears here to be conservative submission to the recorded word of God turns out to be confident assertion of the authority of the living, unwritten word of God's earthly teachers.

This is an extended talmudic deliberation, one which lavishes many words on each detail of the base-Mishnah. The sugya signals its message through repetition—a repetition that is sometimes misplaced and stubborn. As masters of talmudic analysis, we, the readers, are forced to judge the appropriateness of such an unyielding, apparently single-minded voice. When the Mishnah shifts perspective, but the gemara does not follow, and then shifts again, once more to find no echo in the gemara, we will be confused and provoked. By evaluating our own confusion—our need to read the same words in different ways as our focus continues to shift—we will be in a position to formulate interpretations that a nonanalytical reading would likely not admit.

The Mishnah at the end of the first chapter of Ḥagigah remarks:

a. [The laws of] releasing vows hover in the air, and they have nothing [in scripture] on which to depend.
b. The laws of Shabbat, the festival offerings, and the misappropriation of sacred property, lo, they are as mountains hanging from a hair, for they are little scripture and many laws.
c. [The laws of] judgments, and the temple service, and purities and impurities, and forbidden sexual relations, they have something [in scripture] on which to depend—they are the body of Torah.

This Mishnah allows that its laws, reduced to representative categories, have three different relationships to scripture. Some (listed in c) have substantial source in scripture, others (b) originate generally in scripture but have no detailed relationship with its precepts, and still others (a) have no relationship whatsoever with the laws of scripture. Because we would expect a traditional system to claim the profoundest connection with its canonical sources, the latter two categories (b, a) are particularly striking. Not surprisingly, subsequent rabbinic authorities were also troubled by the Mishnah's highlighting of these same categories.

What, precisely, is the trouble? As far as the Mishnah admits, the only source (with rare individual exceptions) of Jewish tradition prior to itself is the Tanakh—the Hebrew Bible. Therefore, when the Mishnah admits that whole categories of its law have little or no source in the Torah, it is saying that this lone, recognized source is not the source of the whole, even by derivation. What other source or sources there might be is not suggested; this problem does not seem to concern this Mishnah. It is content to suggest (in this case, by default) that the only source of its tradition is the teachers whose voices it records. In a larger literary context in which laws of any origin, biblical or not, attributed or unattributed, are presented in the same language and form, this suggests that the primary source and authority of the law of the Mishnah is the Mishnah itself (or its anonymous promulgator), essentially standing outside of any particular context. The voice is, as it were, the voice of eternity, in which what is always was and always will be (again, with only rare exceptions). This eternity, though, is in a profound sense untraditional, for it does not respect the authority of the Torah for the overall scope and definition of its laws. Those laws that do not derive from the Torah are not evidence of change, they just *are*.

The Bavli begins by denying the opinion expressed in the Mishnah's first clause.

a. It is taught: R. Eliezer says, they [the release of vows] do have something [in scripture] to depend on, for it is said "if he should express a vow" (Lev. 27:1), "if he should express a vow" (Num. 6:2) twice—one expression to prohibit and one expression to permit.

b. R. Joshua says: They do have something to depend on, for it is said "whereupon I swore in my anger" (Ps. 95:11), [meaning] in my anger I swore but I have retracted.

c. R. Isaac says: They do have something to depend on, for it is said "[take from them an offering to the Lord,] anyone whose heart is willing" (Exod. 35:5) [meaning that a vow made when the heart is not willing has no effect].

d. Ḥananiah the nephew of R. Joshua says: They do have something to depend on, for it is said, "I have sworn, and I will uphold it, that I will keep your righteous judgments" (Ps. 119:106) [meaning that the upholding of a vow must be willed by the person taking the vow; if it is against that person's will, then the vow is invalid].

e. R. Judah said Samuel said: *If I had been there I would have said*

>   to them—*my [proof] is better than yours*, for it is said "he shall
>   not break his word" (Num. 30:3) [meaning that] he may not
>   break [it] but others may break [it] for him.
>
> f. Rava said: *For all of them there is a refutation except for that of
>   Samuel which has no refutation. . . .* [emphases added]

The refutation of each, showing how each scriptural proof can be read
for another purpose, follows at this point in the gemara.

This first section of the sugya, a baraita followed by two amoraic
opinions, disarms the reader from the very beginning. The four proofs
(a through d) offered by tannaim are all relatively straightforward. Several are upheld elsewhere (in the Yerushalmi's commentary on this
Mishnah and at Bavli Nazir 62a) and there is nothing evident, in their
initial presentation, to suggest that they are problematic. Thus, when
Samuel says that his proof is better than theirs, and Rava strengthens
Samuel's claim by suggesting that the preceding four may all be refuted, the reader is taken aback. We are invited to respond: Do you
mean to say that there is no known tannaitic proof of the law permit-
ting the release of vows? If not, then why do the tannaim quoted here
claim there is? And what does it mean to suggest that amoraim (sages
of the gemara) are able to identify a viable scriptural source when
tannaim were not? Does this mean that, given the knowledge available
in the Mishnaic period, the Mishnah was correct when it said that
these laws have no basis in scripture? Are amoraim correct when they
suggest otherwise? And are they *permitted*, on their own authority, to
take issue with the explicit word of the Mishnah on such a matter?

The tannaim of the baraita, contrary to the Mishnah, strike a blow
for tradition. The amoraim purportedly support the same conclusion,
but only by undermining the tannaim whose conclusion they support.
As we shall see, this same pattern, in which the defense of the traditionality of rabbinic law is at least partially undermined by that same
defense, is repeated throughout the sugya.

The next section of the sugya provides a fine example. With reference to the second clause of the Mishnah ("The laws of Shabbat"),
the Bavli begins by denying the simple claim of the Mishnah:

> g. *The laws of Shabbat.*
> h. They are written!
> i. [This statement of the Mishnah] is needed only for [teaching
>   about] the opinion of R. Abba.

j. For R. Abba said: he who digs a hole on Shabbat and needs only its soil [but not the hole itself] is exempt [from liability] for it [the act of digging].

k. Like whose [opinion is R. Abba's law]?

l. Like R. Shimeon, who said: A labor that is not required for itself [but is done for another purpose, as where the hole is dug not for the hole but for the soil that is extracted], he is exempt [from liability] for it.

m. You might even say [that R. Abba's law follows the opinion of] R. Judah [who said that you are liable for labor that is not required for itself]; there [where he says the offender is liable] he [the offender] improves [through his labor], here [in the case of digging] he damages [and one is not held liable for damaging labor].

n. What is [the phrase] "like mountains hanging from a hair" [referring to]?

o. [To the principle that] the Torah prohibited intended labor

p. and [the principle of] intended labor is not written [in scripture].

The argument of this gemara is that the Mishnah, if understood simply, is wrong, for the laws of Shabbat *are* written (= contained in scripture). However, not wanting to abrogate the Mishnah, the gemara argues that, if understood correctly, the Mishnah's claim is entirely accurate. To accomplish this, the gemara proposes that the true intent of the Mishnah is very limited. Despite the generality of the Mishnah's expression, the gemara would have us believe that, when speaking of Sabbath laws that have little connection to scripture, the Mishnah is referring only to the principle of "labor required for its own purpose" (that is, to be liable for Sabbath work, the intent of the person performing the act must be to benefit directly from the specific labor and not from a by-product of the labor), or, in the latter phrase of the same Mishnaic statement, to the principle of "intended labor." Concerning these categories, says the gemara, the Mishnah is correct. If the Mishnah is limited in this way, the gemara can profess its loyalty to the traditions of both scripture and Mishnah.

But there is a tension here that the reader will have a hard time overlooking. On the one hand, the gemara seeks to make the law of the Mishnah an extension of scripture. The Mishnah will thus be

thoroughly traditional and nothing will have changed from the revelation at Sinai to the present. On the other hand, to preserve the Mishnah, the gemara does admit a "small" exception to the claim that "it
is written," and that exception turns out to be anything but small. The
notion that work must be desired and intended in order to create liability is absolutely central to the rabbinic Sabbath institution.[1] The view
that predominates in rabbinic circles is that any manner of labor, if
performed unintentionally or without desiring the immediate product
of that labor, does not lead to liability. The exception that the Mishnah concerns itself with, therefore, is very significant. Moreover, if it
is not "written," then it must be a bona fide innovation.

This latter point cannot be overemphasized. The Bavli *nowhere* in
this text makes a claim for Oral Torah (though the view is, of course,
expressed elsewhere in the Bavli; see chap. 2). That is to say, there is
no claim here, as there is in the Yerushalmi's commentary on the
same Mishnah, that those laws that are not actually written are nevertheless part of the original revelation. If that revelation is not their
origin, then what is? The Bavli doesn't identify their source, but its
silence is strongly suggestive: if they don't begin at Sinai, they may
well be later creations. Things, apparently, *do* change. On the surface,
there may be denial of this reality ("they are written!"). But careful
examination of the facts shows that the denial is a shaky one.

The next several approaches in the gemara follow virtually the
identical pattern:

Festival offerings.
   a. They are written!
   b. [This statement of the Mishnah] is needed only for that which
      R. Pappa said to Abbaye:
   c. From what [do I know] that this "And you shall celebrate it as a
      ḥag to the Lord" (Exod. 12:14 and Lev. 23:41) [is referring to]
      sacrifice? Maybe the Merciful One is saying "celebrate a fes-
      tival"?
   d. But, if so, that which is written, "hold a feast for me in the
      desert" (Exod. 5:1), is also [saying to] celebrate a festival [without
      bringing sacrifice—the context in Exodus suggests that this is
      not so].
   e. And should you say, indeed, it is so, but is it not written "And
      Moses said: you [Pharaoh] too give into our hands sacrifices and

burnt-offerings" (Exod. 10:25)? [This clearly suggests that sacrifices are intended when the term "celebrate" is used, as it is
above in this same chapter.]

f. Maybe this is what the Merciful One means to say . . .

g. . . .

h. Rather it [the proof that scripture requires sacrifice, and not
mere festivities] comes [by way of a scriptural equation of the
term] "desert" [with] "desert."

i. It is written here, "hold a feast for me in the desert" and it is
written there "the sacrifices and the grain-offering you brought
to me in the desert" (Amos 5:25)—just as there sacrifices [are
meant] so too here sacrifices [are meant].

j. [So, if we have supported the desired conclusion from scripture,]
what is [the meaning of] "mountains hanging from a thread?"
[The rule is that] we do not learn matters of Torah from words
of Tradition [the prophets; in this case, Amos. Therefore,
though the gemara has cleverly proved that "celebrate" means
with a sacrifice, the proof is considered inconclusive].

Again, denying the simple meaning of the Mishnah, the gemara insists that the laws concerning festival offerings (or, to be more precise,
the festival offering, the *hagigah*) *are* written. To save the Mishnah
from error, though, the gemara is forced to find some part of the law
of the festival offering that is not written in scripture. What it identifies
as "not written" (in b through c) is the proof that the Torah, when it
demands "celebration" (using the Hebrew root H-G-G), is speaking of
sacrifice. But this is challenged with the claim that even this *is* written,
and midrashic demonstration of the source of this conclusion in scripture is then offered. Still, in the end, the only convincing proof is said
to come from a scriptural equation with Amos (i), and this is rejected
as invalid; authoritative proof of such a ruling of "Torah" may only
come from the Torah itself. Consequently, we are left without good
scriptural proof of the fact that "celebration" means sacrifice. In this
respect, the Mishnah is correct when it speaks of the laws of festival
sacrifices as "hanging by a hair."

In quality, this approach to the Mishnah is similar to the one preceding it. It claims that the specified laws are written in scripture (contra the Mishnah), it saves the Mishnah by identifying one element of
the law or its construction which is not written, but the element which

is not written turns out to be central to the law as a whole—in this case, literally fundamental. If scripture does not mean sacrifice when it demands "celebrate," then there are no laws of festival sacrifice to discuss! This is more than a mere technicality. If the derivation cannot depend upon the verse from Amos, then, according to the gemara, there is no definitive source for this conclusion. Consequently, the first defensive response to the Mishnah is an empty one. Whatever is "written," the clear and unambiguous demand that a festival sacrifice be brought is not.

As we might expect by this point, the opening words of the gemara's response to the next part of the Mishnah, speaking of the misappropriation of sacred property, are "They are written!" But so too are the opening words of its response to "judgments," "the Temple service," "purities," and so forth (all of which, according to the Mishnah, have "something [in scripture] on which to depend"). Regardless of which part of the Mishnah it is addressing, each stage of the gemara's rhetorical strategy is the same. It begins by declaring that the laws spoken of in the Mishnah *are* written in scripture. It then suggests that there is, in each case, one specific exception. Like the cases described above, these exceptions sometimes turn out to be significant.

I will illustrate by reference to the gemara's commentary on "judgments" and "purities." Each of the gemara's approaches is extremely brief.

Judgments.
    a. They are written!
    b. [The Mishnah's statement] is only necessary for such as [the teaching of] Rabbi [Judah the Patriarch]
    c. for it is taught [in a baraita]: Rabbi says [quoting Exod. 21:23], "soul for soul" [meaning] monetary compensation. Do you say monetary compensation, or is it not [perhaps] literally a soul? "Giving" is said below (Exod. 21:23) and "giving" is said above (Exod. 21:22)—just as there [it means] monetary compensation, so too here [it means] monetary compensation.

[11a] *Purities.*
    a. They are written!
    b. [The Mishnah's statement] is only necessary for the [required legal] measure of a mikveh [ritual bath] which is not written,
    c. for it is taught [in a baraita]: "And he shall wash . . . in water"

(Lev. 15:16), [meaning] in the water of a mikveh, "all of his flesh" (ibid.), [requiring] water which all of his flesh may enter. And how much is this? A cubit by a cubit, with the height of three cubits, and the sages figured the [measure of the] waters of a mikveh at forty seahs.

Briefly, in each of these cases the gemara responds to the Mishnah's observation that these laws "have something on which to depend [in scripture]" by declaring, in effect, "No! They have *more* than something on which to depend. They are actually written!" However, to save the Mishnah, the gemara needs to show that there is, at least, something in the law that is not actually spelled out in detail—that has something to "lean on" but nothing more. In the case of judgments, this "something" is the principle of monetary compensation; in the case of purities, it is the measure of water to be contained in a purifying ritual bath. Needless to say, each of these are crucial to the categories of law here being discussed. In fact, it would be fair to say that in neither case is there a law more central to the categories under discussion than these.

The gemara's generalized strategy, expressed here still again, creates two important problems. First, as we have seen, the exceptions that are admitted undermine the claim for traditionality that opens each commentary. If matters such as the principle of intended labor on Shabbat and the status of the obligation to bring a festival offering are, at best, of dubious scriptural origin, then what value is there to claiming that other laws "are written"? This doesn't change the admission that laws—even important laws—need *not* have been written. Similarly, if a principle such as monetary compensation in the case of damages, or the measure of a mikveh, are not actually written (they must be *derived*; that is, they merely "lean" on scripture), then what force is there to the claim that these laws are written?

Second, the gemara's rhetoric levels the three distinct categories that the Mishnah describes. The second and third of the Mishnah's categories are treated in precisely the same manner, beginning with exactly the same counterclaim, as though the Mishnah's claim about each is the same. There are not three possible relationships of the Mishnah's law to scripture, the gemara says (again, contra the Mishnah)—there is only one: the Mishnah's laws are scriptural (except, of course, for specific exceptions, sometimes significant, which are not).

Ironically, this levelling undermines the Mishnah's characterization of the third category of laws (which, in contrast to the second, has "much scripture" on which to depend) because, in order for the Gemara's response ("They are written!") to be meaningful, we must now read the Mishnah to say "they have something on which to depend [but they are not, in any significant way, actually written; see Rashi, ad. loc.]." To strengthen the overall argument for the traditionality of rabbinic law, the Mishnah's explicit claim for the traditionality of certain categories of law must be weakened. As before in individual details, now the gemara's overall rhetoric strangely undermines its expressed purpose.

The Bavli's desire to erase the categories that the Mishnah constructs is evident in another of its approaches as well. In connection with the Mishnah's general description of the second category ("little scripture and many laws"), the gemara comments (at 11a):

    a. It is taught: Skin afflictions and "tents" [the laws of impurity imparted by a corpse in a closed space] have little scripture and many laws.

    b. Skin afflictions have little scripture?! Skin afflictions have much scripture!! [See Lev. 13–14.]

    c. R. Pappa said: This is what is being said—skin afflictions have much scripture and few laws and "tents" have little scripture and many laws.

    d. And what difference does it make [if there is much or little scripture]?

    e. If you have a doubt regarding a matter of skin afflictions, consult scripture, and if you have a doubt regarding a matter of "tents," consult the Mishnah.

The claim made in (a) (skin afflictions has little scripture) is so absurd that the reader would respond with the objection in (b) even before the gemara has an opportunity to voice it. In fact, it is so patently incorrect that it is difficult to imagine why the gemara wanted to preserve it, only to perform this little corrective exercise, in the first place. As I see it, this small section affects the reader's perceptions in two ways: First, it leads him to be suspicious of categories that are formulated according to these conventions ("much scripture," "few laws," etc.). Not only must he reject the statement of the baraita quoted in (a), he is also now likely to be wary of any such categorization. Second, the response in (e) suggests that there is no truly important difference between these categories in any case. It is all a matter of mechanics; where do you look if you do not know the answer? In the opinion of this gemara, where you look doesn't seem to make a significant difference, for scripture and the Mishnah are both admitted to be authoritative sources of the law.

Ultimately, I think, the gemara's point in leveling the categories is to say that there is no significant difference whether the law comes from scripture or from the rabbis. This same point is likewise communicated in the gemara's various "minor exceptions" to the claim that "it is written." What are these exceptions, after all? In the case of Shabbat, the admitted exception is laws relating to intent in the performance of prohibited labor. For judgments, it is the teaching that "eye for eye" means monetary compensation. For purities, it is the proper measure of a mikveh. Any educated reader would know that, as far as rabbinic understanding of Shabbat law is concerned, the question of intention makes all the difference in the world. In the matter of judgments, he would recognize that nothing could be more basic to rabbinic application of these laws than the principle of monetary compensation. If these things find no strong source in scripture, it hardly matters what does. The reader would immediately recognize this point, and he would likely conclude, therefore, that the gemara's claim that all of these laws "are written" is a relatively empty one. Still, this will have little consequence for, as the gemara itself intimates (and elsewhere records explicitly), all of these laws, whether written explicitly in scripture, derived by the rabbis from scripture or promulgated by the rabbis without a source in scripture, are Torah.

5.

On Truth, Human and Divine

What does it mean to say that rabbinic tradition is "Torah?" If by "Torah" the rabbis mean that it was "all given to Moses at Sinai" (to borrow the language used at Berakhot 5a[1]), then it makes little difference whether any particular word of Torah is Written or rabbinic. If it was all given to Moses at Sinai, it is fundamentally irrelevant what form it later took. But if the sages also admit genuine innovation in the tradition (as the text studied in the preceding chapter seems to imply) or if they view the Oral tradition as imperfect or incomplete—this would make a big difference. If the law is justified on the basis of something other than the authority of Sinai, then our vision of the tradition, as represented by the rabbis, would change significantly. Which is it, then, Sinai or Palestine? Is rabbinic Torah a perfect record of what happened at Sinai, or is it also a product of the struggles of rabbis living in the later Palestine and Babylonia?

The Berakhot tradition referred to earlier (along with noteworthy parallels) suggests that Mishnah and its interpretation were also part of the original revelation of God's complete truth. But the rabbis were aware that their tradition, as they themselves record it, is replete with disputes on any number of matters, from minor to significant. If the entirety of Torah, including the Oral Torah, was given to Moses on Sinai, then how can we explain such differences of opinion? The Tosefta, long before the Bavli, suggests: "When the students of Shammai and Hillel who did not serve [their masters] as necessary increased, disputes [also] increased in Israel and two Torahs were created" (Hag. 2:9, Sot. 14:9 [2]). Thus, whatever the original status of the Oral tradition, its condition during the rabbinic age is vastly transformed. According to this view of the Tosefta, a view repeated in the Yerushalmi and Bavli, ancient perfection has been supplanted by error and dispute.

Where does this leave the rabbis in late antiquity? How do the Bavli's authors understand *their* Torah? Is it a perfect original or an imperfect distortion? Is it a full realization of God's truth, or an imperfect product of human processes? These are not questions that can go unanswered. Their answers will tell us whether rabbis are mere defenders of the faith, as it were, or the autonomous shapers of a new-old tradition.

The text we will use to explore the rabbis' answers to these questions—at least in their latest classical formulation—is the sugya at Eruvin 13b. Unlike the texts studied in chapters 3 and 4, this one limits the scope of its discussion greatly, communicating its views in the play of the finest details. We must therefore read this sugya in all of its particulars, listening to the dialogue of each voice with the one before it. Here, again, I will suggest that the deliberation argues against itself in meaningful ways. But the text also makes its points directly, and the combination of expressed opinion and intimation, artfully combined to compose a clear and well-developed argument, will allow us to interpret with confidence the ultimate lesson of the text at hand.

The first part of the sugya follows.

a. R. Aḥa b. Ḥanina said: It is revealed and known before "The One Who spoke and the world came into being" that there is none in the generation of R. Meir who is comparable to him, and for what reason [then] did they not fix the law according to him? Because his colleagues could not comprehend the fullness of his opinion, for he would say for [that which is actually] impure "pure," and give it reason, and say for [that which is actually] pure "impure," and give it reason.

b. It is taught [in a baraita]: His name is not really R. Meir, but R. Nehorai.[3] And why is he called R. Meir? Because he enlightens (*"me'ir"*) the eyes of sages with halakha. . . .

c. Rabbi[4] said: The fact that I am sharper than my colleagues is

because I saw R. Meir from the rear, and had I seen him from
the front I would have been [even] sharper, for it is written,
"and your eyes shall see your teacher" (Isa. 30:20).

d. R. Abbahu said R. Yohanan said: R. Meir had a student by the
name of Symmachus who would, for each and every impure
thing, give forty-eight reasons for its impurity, and for each and
every pure thing [he would give] forty-eight reasons for its
purity.

e. It is taught [in a baraita]: There was an experienced student in
Yavne who would purify the crawling creature [who is explicitly
declared impure in the Torah; see Lev. 11:29–38] with one
hundred and fifty reasons.

f. Ravina[5] said: I will make a deduction and purify it. And if a
snake, which kills and [thereby] increases impurity, is pure
[when it dies], a crawling creature, which does not [ordinarily]
kill and increase impurity, how much the more so [should it
be pure].

g. And it is not so, [for] it [the snake] is merely doing the act of a
thorn [that is, the snake is a natural force and should no more
be counted impure for what is causes than a thorn].

Let us read this text step by small step. To begin with, R. Meir is
spoken of as being without rival in his generation because he can
skillfully demonstrate that what is impure is pure, and what is pure is
impure. The reader recoils in puzzlement; why, in a society in which
matters of purity and impurity are so important, would such a skill be
praised? One might well think that the opposite would be true—that
such a skill should be condemned! Yet that is clearly not the case
here. The reader's confusion is compounded in the very next step, in
which Meir is spoken of as "enlightening the eyes of the sages with
halakha" (b) despite the fact that Meir's colleagues do not understand
his subtleties, as we learned in the first step. How do these two seemingly contradictory claims work? In which direction do we reconcile
the tensions the sugya lays out at the very beginning?

The next step (c) suggests a direction, though (as we shall see) a
fantastic and surprising one. Now we learn that the very sight of R.
Meir would make someone sharper, as confirmed by the case of Meir's
student Symmachus, who could give so many reasons for the purity
or impurity of given things (d). Of course, this latter testimony shows

that, despite Meir's ability to confuse matters of purity and impurity through reasoned argument, his students (or, at least, some of his students) knew what was really pure or impure and could give ample explanations of their rulings. Still, because of R. Meir's ability convincingly to argue the opposite of the truth, his view in the law was not generally accepted.

These latter steps make it clear that, despite the potentially perverse consequences of R. Meir's method, the sugya intends to offer him the highest of praises. In fact, if we account for the allusions built into this section, we will appreciate that the praise is even more extraordinary than our preliminary synopsis would suggest. Step (c) contains an unmistakable allusion to the story of Moses and God at "the cleft of the rock" (Exod. 33:22). There, the reader will recall, the issue is Moses' viewing of God, and God permits Moses to see God's back but not God's front. God passes before Moses (who sees God's back), and then commands Moses to write a second set of the Tablets of the Law (the first set having been broken when Moses descended from the mountain the first time only to witness the worship of the Golden Calf). Soon thereafter, Moses descends with the new set of tablets, his face shining as a result of coming into the presence of God.

The parallel elements are clear: the viewing of the back, the hope to view the front, the effect on the one who views, the lighting or enlightening by the lawgiver. What is striking, though, about these allusions is the confusion of reference. On the one hand, when Meir is said to improve the wit of students who see his front, he takes the position of God in the Torah's story. It is Meir's back, like God's, that may be/has been seen. It is Meir's presence, like God's, that enlightens others. On the other hand, when Meir "lightens"/gives light to others, he resembles Moses, whose face shines when he descends with the law. Which, then, is it? Is Meir meant to be equated with Moses or with God? I would argue that it makes little difference. In fact, the tension of the ambiguity makes the literary hyperbole more effective than it might otherwise be. At this stage, we need merely understand that Meir the lawgiver/transmitter-of-the-law, as though standing at Sinai, may *not* be relied upon as the direct source of the law, for his Torah (like the Torah of Sinai?) is too brilliant.

Still, the text does claim that Meir produces students such as Symmachus, who could get the law straight. Is this, then, the praiseworthy quality of R. Meir—that, however indirect his method, his students seem to learn the difference between pure and impure? Perhaps. But such an outcome is not emphasized (nor, for that matter, even mentioned) in what follows, and what is emphasized instead is the skill to do as R. Meir does—that is, to reason against halakha. Moreover, it becomes clear as the sugya progresses that this is a capability that is highly valued. The baraita quoted in (e) teaches approvingly of a student who could, through careful and abundant reasoning, argue for the purity of something that the Torah itself explicitly declares to be impure. Ravina (or Rav or Rava) then boasts that he can do the same, giving at least one reason for the desired (perverse) conclusion. The gemara, though, rejects his argument (g), easily showing that his reasoning is flawed. Then, in the next section (quoted below), the text shifts its focus slightly, forcing us to ask the meaning of the partial closure accomplished in this latter step.

Why does the gemara quote this hollow boast of Ravina, only to reject it? In the gemara to this point, the capability to make pure impure, and vice versa, has been praised several times. The fact that such individuals as R. Meir, the student at Yavne, and, now, Ravina undertake this exercise shows how praiseworthy such cleverness is in the eyes of the present authors. There is something valuable in the sharpness of reason, even when playfully turned against the halakhic tradition. The play of alternatives is a demonstration of excellence, and the more alternatives, the more excellent is the Torah that one teaches. Against this background, the failure of Ravina's *single* alternative takes on marked significance. Consider: On the basis of the prior step, we might have concluded that the ability to twist the law this way is not all that rarified. If some anonymous "experienced student" can offer one hundred and fifty reasons to purify the crawling creature (!), then how difficult could it be? The answer, provided by this next step of the gemara (f), is "very difficult." Ravina (or Rav or Rava; the different versions do not change the point here) is perhaps the outstanding rabbinic sage of his generation. If even he cannot provide *a single* reason for purifying the crawling creature, then it must be a difficult exercise indeed! It is an expression of rare brilliance, a brilliance which, though technically perverse, is to be praised above other qualities. What is more important, this text asks, brilliance or accurate delineation of the halakha? The present answer, to be supported from a different perspective below, is *not* accurate delineation of the halakha.

To put this latter observation in a slightly different way, we may say that this text distinguishes, clearly and unambiguously, between practice and study, between rabbinic law and divine truth. It declares that the determination of divine truth—meaning the single, decisive, clear truth of God's will—is not the point. There is no other way to explain its insistence that arguing even against explicit rulings of the Torah is valuable. Though it might often be difficult to ascertain precisely what the Torah means, it should not be difficult to conclude that an opinion that obviously and directly contradicts a law of the Torah ("pig is kosher") cannot possibly be a part of divine truth. But, we are told here, even such opinions are worth offering and pursuing. For reasons not yet spelled out, even views that appear to be patently untrue (contrary to God's expressed will) should be explored.

Attention to the question of God's "truth" (God's expressed will) and its relation to rabbinic law, an issue already coming to the fore above, will explain the next turn of the gemara.

h. R. Abba b. Samuel⁶ said: For three years the School of Shammai and the School of Hillel disputed, these saying "the law is like us" and these saying "the law is like us." A heavenly voice emerged and said "[Both] these and these are the words of the living God, and the law is according to the School of Hillel."

i. Now, being that "these and these are the words of the living God," why did the School of Hillel merit having the law fixed according to them?

j. Because they were pleasing and humble, and they taught their own words and the words of the School of Shammai, and not only that, but they [even] gave priority to the words of the School of Shammai before their own words,

k. like that which we have taught [in m. Suk. 2:7]: He whose head and most of whose body were in the sukkah, but his [dinner] table was in the house, the School of Shammai declare this unfit and the School of Hillel declare it fit. The School of Hillel said to the School of Shammai—"Wasn't the case thus, that the elders of the School of Shammai and the elders of the School of Hillel went to visit R. Yohanan b. Ha-horanit and found him sitting with his head and most of his body in the sukkah and his table in the house!" The School of Shammai said to them—"Is that a proof?! Even did they say to him: If this is how you have practiced, you have never in your days fulfilled the commandment of sukkah!"

l. [This story is intended] to teach you that, anyone who lowers himself, the Holy One, Blessed be He, raises him, whereas anyone who raises himself, the Holy One, Blessed be He, lowers him; and anyone who pursues greatness, greatness flees from him, whereas anyone who flees from greatness, greatness seeks him; and anyone who "presses the hour" [seeks to achieve wealth or greatness before his time], the hour presses him, whereas anyone who is pushed aside for the hour, the hour will stand for him [and he will succeed in the appropriate time].

m. Our sages taught [in a baraita]: For two and a half years, the School of Shammai and the School of Hillel disputed, these saying "it would have been better if man had not been created than been created," and these saying "it would have been better if [= it is better that] man had been created than not been created." They voted and decided "it would have been better if man had not been created than been created, but now that he has been created he should examine his actions. . . ."

The tradition of Abba b. Samuel (h, perhaps quoting an earlier tradition; cf. y. Yebamot 1:6, 3*b* and parallels) declares that, even in disputes where diametrically opposed opinions are offered, "these and these are the words of the living God." How odd! How can contradictory opinions *both* be the "words of the living God?" If either of the opinions held the whole truth—the perfect realization of God's will— then this evaluation would be absurd. Obviously, therefore, neither the opinion of the School of Shammai nor that of the School of Hillel can contain God's truth fully. Only if this is so may both be spoken of as the Word of God.

Against this background, the gemara barely needs ask its next question (i)—if both are "the words of the living God," why was the law fixed in accordance with the views of Hillel? Yet, as though to emphasize its awareness of the logical problem it has just created, the gemara makes the question explicit, and offers a disarmingly humanistic response: the law follows the Hillelites because (1) they were pleasing and (2) humble and (3) they taught the Shammaite opinions along with their own and (4) they even gave priority to the Shammaite views. The first two parts of the answer are striking for what they are not: no

claim is made that the Hillelites are more brilliant than the Shammaites. No one argues that their record of the tradition is superior.
Rather, what makes the Hillelites superior is their special human qualities. What matters, at this stage of the answer in any case, is not their
relationship to God and God's revelation but their relationship to other
human beings.

The matter of God's revelation comes up, by intimation at least, in
the latter part of the answer. The positions of the Hillelites are preferred, we learn, because they teach the positions of the School of
Shammai along with their own, and they even give priority to the
positions of their opponents! Why is such an approach so praiseworthy? Because it speaks for the recognition that no opinion or interpretation fully contains the truth of God's revealed will, and therefore
alternatives must always be offered. The Shammaites, who presumably taught only their own views—otherwise their opinions too could
have become halakha—did not recognize this essential fact. The Hillelites, admitting that some part of God's truth could be found even
in contradictory views, merited the fixing of halakha in accordance
with their admittedly less-than-true opinions.

Despite this one important shortcoming in the School of Shammai—their failure to look beyond their own opinions—the context
provided by this gemara suggests that their opinion is not in other
ways to be considered inferior. We recall that this lengthy deliberation
commenced with a question involving "fixing the halakha in accordance with. . . ." We learned at (a) that the law was not fixed in
accordance with the views of R. Meir "because his colleagues could
not comprehend the fullness of his opinion. . . ." Here (at i through
j) it is the Shammaites who stand in the position of Meir (not having
the halakha fixed in accordance with their opinion). So, though the
Hillelites might be humble and understanding, we are led by association to conclude that the Shammaites are brilliant and clever. If this
is correct, we must assume that, though neither Shammai nor Hillel
may capture the fullness of God's truth, Shammai and his followers
are likely to approximate it more often than Hillel and his followers.
Yet, we know, the law follows the opinion of the School of Hillel,
regardless of its objective accuracy. We see again that God's will (as
recorded in Torah) and rabbinic law evidently are less than likely to
coincide.

In its next step, (k), the gemara quotes a Mishnah to illustrate the point already made in (j), that is, the qualities on the basis of which Hillel is preferred in halakha. But the demonstration is problematic in a variety of ways. First, it is not clear how the quoted Mishnah shows that the School of Hillel "were pleasing and humble, and they taught their own words and the words of the School of Shammai, and not only that, but they [even] gave priority to the words of the School of Shammai before their own words." Rashi suggests, weakly, that when the Hillelites address the Shammaites by saying "Wasn't the case thus, that the elders of the School of Shammai and the elders of the school of Hillel . . . ," it shows that they gave priority to the words of the School of Shammai. But there are no "words" here to be given priority. This is a narrative, given in an explicitly rhetorical context, and not the representation of different opinions in the law. Rashi admits as much in his comment on the previous part of the tradition ("they taught their own words and the words of the School of Shammai") when, rather than looking for illustration to the Sukkah Mishnah quoted here, he looks to another example entirely. He also seems to feel that there is no clear evidence here of the Hillelites teaching both their own words and those of the School of Shammai. Putting Rashi's interpretation aside, we might suggest that the gemara assumes that the Mishnah itself derives from the School of Hillel (as, ultimately, it indeed does). The fact that this Mishnah teaches both opinions should therefore be taken as evidence of Hillelites giving priority to the words of Shammai and his school. But, as Rashi's comment shows, this is at best unclear. Furthermore, if any Mishnah that quotes the opinion of both schools could have been given in evidence, then the choice of the present Mishnah is particularly puzzling.

As it happens, this Mishnah, quoted to prove why the law follows the opinions of the School of Hillel, is one of the few cases where the law actually follows the Shammaites. As we read the exchange in the Mishnah, we are struck by the fact that when the Shammaites respond to the attempted proof of the Hillelites, the Hillelites appear to have no rejoinder; it appears reasonable, therefore, that the law must follow the School of Shammai. The Yerushalmi indeed takes this to be so, and for other reasons the Bavli also supports the Shammaite view (b. Suk. 3a). It is, we must admit, rather odd to demonstrate the halakhic preference for the Hillelite view by using a text that both talmudim agree demonstrates the opposite! What possible reason could there be for doing so?

The answer, I think, is again to moderate claims for a definitive halakha or for the necessary connection between rabbinic legal tradition and divine truth. As the Mishnah quoted here illustrates, exceptions are plentiful and alternatives are often available. In most cases, the decided law is not even likely to be the best approximation of God's revealed will. Furthermore, even the "truth" of a systemic rule such as "the law follows the School of Hillel" should not be taken for granted. For various reasons, including their possibly greater theoretical brilliance (see Yevamot 14a, discussed in chapter 6), the School of Shammai might still, from time to time, emerge on top.

The sugya (at m) concludes by recapitulating this same point in another connection. Perhaps in order to emphasize that halakha is only a part of its concern, the text quotes a dispute between the schools of Hillel and Shammai that has nothing to do with the legal side of rabbinic teachings. The question is whether the creation of humankind was a good thing or not, the negative opinion apparently being associated with the Shammaites and the positive with the Hillelites. (We conclude this because the Shammaites and the negative opinion are both mentioned first, and the Hillelites and the positive opinion are mentioned second. The general sense of the personalities of the two schools and their founders would also lead us to make this association.) It turns out, though, that the negative view, associated with the Shammaites, is the accepted one, and so at the end—notwithstanding halakhic preference to the contrary—the Shammaites emerge victorious.

The victory is a disturbing one. Not only does the conclusion as stated negate the essential goodness of human existence, it impeaches the wisdom of the God who created us. In other words, if it would have been better that we not have been created, then God must have been wrong to create us. How are we to understand this conclusion? How does it relate to what comes before?

Evidently, there is a divine truth and a human truth, truths that stand independent of each other. Human reason may not grasp divine truth, but, the sugya concludes, the conclusions of human reason need not be negated on this account. On the contrary, in connection with so fundamental a question as the wisdom of creation, human reason may triumph. Somehow, the divine choice might be the wrong one. As we come to understand this, we are left confused and troubled, with the sense that there is no clear, correct answer. Recalling the lessons of the earlier parts of the sugya, we recognize that we can predict neither what will be accepted nor what rejected, which view will be convincing nor which closer to the truth. Truth and practice—divine truth and human truth—do not necessarily align. Consequently, it is an essential act of Torah to pursue many opinions. Human reason is worthy of examination even if it contradicts Torah; how much more so if it contains part of the Torah's truth.

If this reading is correct (that is, if it may be defended as reasonable based upon the signals of the text), then we may conclude that the separation of scripture and tradition, as noted in earlier chapters, is well understood—and even supported—by the rabbinic authors of the Bavli. In the company of their intended readers, at least, they do not hesitate to admit this distance; in fact, they may even be said to celebrate it. To allude to a rabbinic insight suggested in another well-known talmudic text, this community of readers understands that, once God's law was published (in the Torah), God gave up control of its interpretation. It was no longer "in Heaven," and thus the majority of earthly voices would rule (see B.M. 59b). The necessary outcome of such a condition was that decisions would have to rely upon something more mundane than the "truth" of any given interpretation. Hence the success of this view of Hillel and his followers. Hence the success of rabbinic Judaism in the long term.

6.

Pluralism
and Pragmatism

If it is true that there is a gap between God's will as recorded in Written Torah and rabbinic application as recorded in Oral Torah, then this may (or may not) have consequences in practice. If the rabbis recognized and admitted this reality, as I argued in chapter 5, then they would be forced to consider the problem of unity or diversity in community norms. Multiple opinions are the inevitable result of imperfect interpretive processes. Are alternatives to be suppressed in practice, as the heavenly decision in favor of Hillel might suggest, or is there room for multiplicity not only in theory (the evidence for which is found on every page of Talmudic deliberation) but in practice as well? If my readings of prior texts approach the truth of rabbinic perception, then this is a question that cannot be avoided.

Let me specify the considerations on both sides. "Intellectual honesty" might demand that, if alternative opinions are more or less equally (im)perfect, then each opinion must be respected in practice. Because each position is supported "for the sake of Heaven"—because each is motivated by its advocate's belief that it is the best realization of God's will—then how could the rabbinic community demand adherence to an alternative? From the position of a person who supports opinion A but not opinion B, B is at best mistaken and at worst sinful! How, even for the sake of unity, could advocates of B demand such a compromise of personal convictions?

On the other hand, halakhic practice (unlike talmudic theory) is a concern of the social realm, in which differences in practice might well destroy the unity or cohesion of Jewish society. One could therefore argue—and one might expect the rabbis to conclude—that social realities demand relative uniformity of practice even when theoretical disagreements might lead in different directions. As theorists, the rabbis could allow themselves relatively wide latitude, but as religious leaders concerned for the welfare of Jewish society, they might reasonably decide to limit options—to demand adherence to a common set of practices and regulations.

The sugya that addresses these questions at greatest length is found at Yebamot 13b–14b, against the background of a Mishnah that declares:

> Even though these permit and these prohibit,[1] these declare unfit and these declare fit, the School of Shammai did not avoid marrying women of the [community of the] School of Hillel, nor did the School of Hillel [avoid marrying women of the community of] the School of Shammai.

If the Mishnah may be taken at its word, the rabbinic community exercised latitude in practice yet did not allow differences of practice to divide the community. The question for the gemara, therefore, will be whether the Mishnah can be taken at its word. Were such differences actually put into practice, as the Mishnah seems to imply, or does the fact that the two communities continued to intermarry suggest that their differences remained at the level of theory? As an interpretive exercise, these are the choices the gemara will be forced to confront.

This sugya takes the form of a typical halakhic deliberation. But, as the following analysis shows, attention to halakha, following common talmudic conventions, has implications that far transcend "mere" halakha. Our attentiveness to the rhetoric of the sugya will show how the rabbis employ common talmudic approaches to sway the student's/reader's attitudes and opinions in ways that are entirely unexpected.

The sugya begins with a discussion of the mitzvah directive "do not separate yourselves into factions" (based upon a fanciful reading of Deut. 14:1):

> a. We taught there [in m. Meg. 1:1]: The megillah [Scroll of Esther] is read on the eleventh and on the twelfth and on the

thirteenth and on the fourteenth and on the fifteenth [days of the month of Adar], not before and not after.

b. Resh Laqish said to R. Yoḥanan: I will read [and apply] here "don't make incisions [*lo titgodedu*]" (Deut. 14:1) [meaning, through a fanciful misreading of the Hebrew root,] don't make factions . . .

c. He said to him: And to this point have you not learned [the Mishnah of Pesaḥim 4:1 that teaches] "[In] a place where they were accustomed to do work on the day before Passover until midday, they do so, [and in] a place where they are accustomed not to do [work] they do not do so." [Obviously, therefore, it is legitimate for different parts of the Jewish community to conduct themselves differently.]

d. He said to him: I said to you a [matter of bona fide] prohibition

e. . . .

f. and you said to me [a matter of mere] custom!

g. And there [in the case of Passover] is it not [also] a [matter of] prohibition? And have we not learned [in m. Pesaḥim 4:5]: "The nighttime [of the day before Passover], the School of Shammai prohibit and the School of Hillel permit."

h. He said to him: There the one who sees [a person following the opinion of the School of Shammai and not working] says that he has no work. [This does not appear as an act of factiousness, therefore.]

i. But [we learn in the Mishnah here in Yevamot] the School of Shammai permit the co-wives [of the deceased] to [marry] the [surviving] brothers and the School of Hillel prohibit. . . . [These differences of marriage law would clearly create different factions!]

The issue to be addressed in this gemara, raised in (b), is whether the Jewish community is permitted (according to rabbinic law) to divide itself into "factions," that is, to practice the law according to different opinions in different parts of the community. This principle is raised in objection to the law of Mishnah Megillah 1:1, which records that different sorts of communities read the Scroll of Esther to celebrate the holiday of Purim on different days of the month of Adar. R. Yoḥanan, surprisingly, responds to the problem raised by Resh Laqish (in b) not by answering it but by saying, in effect, "And is this the first time you have noticed the problem? There are other prominent examples of such 'factionalism' as well!" (see c). Resh Laqish tries to explain why the problem he raised was the more difficult one (d through f). But his proposed distinction fails and, in the last step we have seen, the gemara draws our attention to what is potentially the most serious "factionalism" of all—a difference of opinion regarding marriage law which, if carried into practice, would mean that certain marriages permitted in one part of the community will be prohibited in another part. Can a community live with such differences? The problem will not go away.

Having touched upon a difference with the gravest of potential consequences, the gemara immediately goes on to consider the (safer) possibility that the many theoretical differences of opinion recorded in rabbinic tradition were never put into practice. The extended discussion follows.

    j. Do you think the School of Shammai acted on the basis of their opinions? The School of Shammai did not act on the basis of their opinions.

    k. And R. Yoḥanan said, "They certainly did!"

    l. And [they are engaged] in the [same] dispute as Rav and Samuel, for Rav says, "The School of Shammai did not act on the basis of their opinions," and Samuel says, "They certainly did!"

    m. When [does this dispute apply]?

    n. If you say [that they are arguing about the period] before the heavenly voice [in Yavne announced that the law follows the School of Hillel], then what is the reason of the one who says they did not act [why not, being that no heavenly decision had yet been made]?

    o. But if after the heavenly voice, then what is the reason of the one who says they did act [being that the heavenly voice had already decided against Shammai]?

    p. If you wish, I will say [that the dispute applies to the period] before the heavenly voice, and if you wish, I will say [to the period] after the heavenly voice.

    q. If you wish, I will say before the heavenly voice, and in a case in which the School of Hillel is the majority. [Under those conditions] the one who says [the School of Shammai] did not act [on the basis of their opinions says so] because the School of Hillel were the majority [and the law generally follows the majority]. And the one who says that they did act [says this because] we go according to the majority only when [the competing parties] are equivalent, but here [the gemara posits] the School of Shammai are "sharper."

r. And if you wish, I will say after the heavenly voice. The one who says they did not act [says this] because the heavenly voice had come out [and announced a decision]. And the one who says they did act, it is R. Joshua['s opinion that he follows], for he said that we pay no heed to a heavenly voice.

The question, following upon the gemara's observation that different practices may endanger the unity of the community, is whether the School of Shammai actually followed their opinions in practice. This question is complicated by two facts: (1) a heavenly voice at Yavne (late first century) declared that the law follows the Hillelites, and (2) even before the heavenly voice, it is assumed that the Hillelites were in the majority and that the law should therefore follow them. With great deftness, the gemara shows that the School of Shammai could in fact have followed their opinions in practice, both before and subsequent to the Yavnean revelation. The problem of community unity remains in place, so the gemara goes on to address this issue once again:

s. And the one who said they did act, why do we not read here *"lo titgodedu"* (Deut. 14:1), meaning "don't separate yourselves into factions?"

t. Abbaye said: We say *"lo titgodedu"* only with respect to two courts in one city, these teaching according to the opinions of the School of Shammai and these teaching according to the opinions of the School of Hillel, but [with respect to] two courts in two cities, we have no objection.

u. Rava said to him: But the School of Shammai and the School of Hillel are as two courts in one city [and, according to the opinion currently being explored, they legitimately put their differing opinions into practice under these conditions].

v. Rather, Rava said: We only say *"lo titgodedu"* with respect to a court in one city, in which half teach in accordance with the School of Shammai and half teach in accordance with the

School of Hillel, but [with respect to] two courts in one city, we have no objection.

Two solutions are offered, one more moderate (Abbaye) and one more radical (Rava). According to both, the prohibition "don't make factions" is restricted to relatively limited circumstances, and there is thus no necessary contradiction between the prohibition and rabbinic pluralism. Still, the gemara is not yet satisfied. It goes on to challenge:

w. Come and hear [an objection]: "In R. Eliezer's place they would, on Shabbat, cut the wood to make the coals to make the iron [to make the knife to perform the circumcision of a boy born on the previous Shabbat]; in the place of R. Jose the Galilean they would eat fowl with milk." In R. Eliezer's place they would [do so, but] in R. Aqiba's place they would not, for, it is taught [in m. Shab. 19:1], "R. Aqiba stated a general rule: Any labor that it is possible to do before Shabbat does not supersede Shabbat." [This objection is directed, as the response in the following step makes clear, against the opinion that claims that the School of Shammai did not act on the basis of their opinions—i.e., "don't subdivide into factions."]

x. What sort of objection is this? [Haven't we already learned that, even according to the more restrictive interpretation of "*lo titgodedu*,"] different places are different [and are not subject to the prohibition of factionalism]?

y. And the one who taught it [the objection], why did he teach it [seeing that it was obviously not a good objection]?

z. You might have thought that, on account of the severity of Shabbat, [the whole world] is like a single place; [this case delineated in w] comes to teach us [otherwise].[2]

aa. Come and hear [another objection]: R. Abbahu, when he went to R. Joshua b. Levi's place he would handle a lamp [on Shabbat, despite the fact that the kindling of the lamp would have been prohibited], but when he went to R. Yohanan's place he would not handle a lamp.

bb. And so what is the problem? Do we not say that different places are different [and not subject to the prohibition of factionalism]?

cc. This is what we are saying: How could R. Abbahu have acted this way in this place and that way in that place?

dd. R. Abbahu was of the [same] opinion as R. Joshua b. Levi [who permitted], and when he went to R. Yoḥanan's place he would not handle [a lamp] because of R. Yoḥanan's honor.

ee. But isn't there his attendant [who, seeing R. Abbahu's contradictory actions and not understanding the reason, might become confused]?

ff. He informed his attendant.

gg. Come and hear [a final objection]: "Even though these prohibit and these permit, the School of Shammai did not refrain from marrying women of the School of Hillel, nor did the School of Hillel [avoid] those of the School of Shammai (m. Yebamot 1:4)."

hh. It is fine if you say that [the School of Shammai] did not act [on the basis of their opinions], for this reason they did not avoid [intermarrying]. But if you say that they did act, why did they not avoid [intermarrying]?

ii. [At this point the Gemara establishes that the schools of Shammai and Hillel agree on the definition of a mamzer—a child of blemished status whom another nonmamzer Israelite may not marry—and that, in the present dispute, the School of Shammai would be producing children whom the School of Hillel would consider to be mamzerim.]

jj. So do we not learn from this that they did not act [on the basis of their opinions, seeing that they did intermarry? This must mean that the mamzerim whom they might in theory have been producing were not being produced in fact].

kk. No! They certainly did act [on the basis of their opinions. How so?] They informed them [in cases where there were problems] and they separated [in only such instances].

ll. This also makes sense, for it is taught in the end [of the same Mishnah]: "All of the pure things and all of the impure things that these [one school] would purify and these [the other school] would declare impure, [nevertheless] they would not avoid handling their pure things together." If you say, fine, they informed them [when there were problems], for this reason they did not avoid [doing these things together]. But if

> you say they did not inform them [of problems, how could they have done this together]. . . .

mm.   . . . Rather, is it not [obvious] that they informed them? Learn from it!

nn.   [This step briefly shows why the latter part of the Mishnah was a more obvious proof of "they informed them" than the former.]

In order to appreciate the full impact of the Bavli's argument, it is useful to consider how this same problem was handled in other rabbinic circles. The Yerushalmi (Yeb. 1:6, 3b) begins its deliberation on this issue by quoting a baraita (Tosefta 1:10) that clarifies the severity of the halakhic differences between the schools of Hillel and Shammai, yet speaks of the great peace that existed between them. The Yerushalmi gemara, however, objects ("there is the condition of mamzer between them, and yet you say this!?") and proceeds to list several possible solutions, all of which restrict or eliminate the possibility that the Shammaites acted on the basis of their opinions. Finally, the gemara twice declares that the law follows the Hillelites.

Though it begins with a tolerant tradition, the whole thrust of the Yerushalmi is to eliminate the option of tolerance. This is clear both in the nature of the solutions that it quotes and in its emphatic conclusion—the law follows Hillel. The tolerant position of the Mishnah is, in the end, annulled, and the declaration of a single definitive law rests secure.

In contrast, the argument of the Bavli favors toleration. This is suggested, first, in the overall direction of the text. Contrary to the Yerushalmi, the Bavli begins with intolerance ("you shall not separate into factions") and concludes with tolerance. Whereas the Yerushalmi raises the mamzer objection almost immediately, explicit mention of this problem waits, in the Bavli, to the very end (ii), there only to be resolved (kk). And the tradition affirming the heavenly decision in favor of the Hillelites, which so resoundingly concludes the Yerushalmi's deliberation, is never quoted explicitly in the Bavli. When it is, however, referred to (n through r), the potential impact of such a reference is immediately nullified, the text preferring to support a view that ignores heavenly voices.

By setting the context for the opinions of Abbaye and Rava that follow, it is the unattributed section of the sugya, which asks whether and when the Shammaites actually followed their opinions (j through r), that is the key to the argument of the text as a whole. The gemara begins by showing that there were prominent talmudic sages of various generations on both sides of the "did the Shammaites practice?" question. Our recognition that the dispute was ongoing, and that no less important figures than Samuel and R. Yoḥanan believed that the Shammaites *did* practice their opinions, demands that we admit the theoretical legitimacy of such a possibility. The question becomes, simply, when would this condition have been legitimate?

It is fair to say, I think, that the Talmud's reader could be expected to know the tradition of the heavenly voice at Yavne that tilted the halakhic scales in favor of Hillel. Therefore, even without articulating the question ("When does this dispute apply?"), the reader will likely have interpreted the dispute in j through l as referring to the historical past, the period before the declaration of the heavenly voice. When else, after all, could Shammaite practice have been justified? Still, the gemara points out, a problem remains, for before the heavenly voice there is no apparent reason the Shammaites should *not* have followed their opinions, as Rav and R. Yoḥanan's disputants (Samuel and, apparently, Resh Laqish) believe. Needless to say, the reader will have an even harder time understanding the dispute as referring to the period after the heavenly voice. But no option is without its difficulties.

Yet, remarkably, the gemara proceeds to answer its question by proposing—in stereotypical talmudic fashion—that the dispute can be understood as referring to the era either before *or after* the declaration of the heavenly voice (the surprise of this answer, coupled with the precise way it is justified, serves to emphasize how radical are the possibilities the Bavli is here willing to consider!). How can this be so? If it is referring to the earlier era, then the dispute must assume that even then the School of Hillel constituted the majority. Therefore, because rules of rabbinic procedure declare that the law follows the majority, the party who holds that the Shammaites *did not* follow their views can easily justify himself: the law followed the majority (Hillel)! The party who holds that they *did* follow their views, on the other hand, must believe that the rule of the majority applies only where both disputants are equally insightful; if the minority is "sharper," as is claimed here (q), then they may nevertheless follow their own opinions.

The effect of this definition is—both technically and in terms of content—startling. First of all, it turns the burden of proof on its head. Before the heavenly voice, the one who argued that the Shammaites followed their opinions should have needed no justification. But by introducing the consideration of majority-minority (majority rules!) and by positing that the Hillelites were in the majority, it is, all of a sudden, the one who says that the Shammaites did act in accordance with their opinions who must defend himself. Of course, by this reversal the defense is rendered more difficult, and any effective defense is rendered that much more notable. And what a defense, indeed! The position is justified by the claim that the Shammaites were "sharper" (keener) than the Hillelites. This means that the heavenly voice would not finally support the sharper party—that is, the party that was more likely to be "correct"—and, furthermore, that rabbinic Jews had for many centuries, by this point (that is, the time of the composition of the gemara), been following the views of the less "sharp" party (!).

The second part of the gemara's analysis is no less bold. If the dispute pertains to the era following the heavenly declaration that the law follows Hillel, then, of course, those who hold that the Shammaites did not act on the basis of their opinions need no justification. But what of those who claim they did? The affirmative opinion, the gemara suggests, follows the view of R. Joshua, who, in the well-known story of the oven of Akhnai (b. B.M. 59b), declares that the law is "not in heaven" and that heavenly voices, therefore, need not be heeded. This, to be sure, is the definitive conclusion of that story, and it is apparently the stronger conclusion of the analysis here.

But, though apparently solving the problem of the party who believes the Shammaites did put their opinions into practice even after the heavenly voice, a difficulty remains. Whether or not the Hillelites constituted the majority of the community before Yavne, there can be little question that they were the majority after Yavne. Thus, whether we listen to heavenly voices or not, the post-Yavnean law should still have followed the Hillelites because *they were the majority*. A justification of post-Yavnean Shammaite practice therefore requires not only the principle of R. Joshua (we do not heed heavenly voices) but also the principle articulated *for the first and only time* above, that when the minority is keener than the majority, the minority ignore the majority and continue to follow their own opinions.

At this point, the ruling expressed at the beginning of the sugya—don't make factions—would appear to have been radically undermined. For this reason, the next task of the gemara is to "save" the halakha prohibiting factions in the face of those who believe "[the Shammaites] did act [in accordance with their opinions]." But first it is necessary to understand how radical are the consequences of the preceding steps. There are two principles that, perhaps more than any, serve as the foundations of the rabbinic halakhic system. The first, which is a historical fact as much as a principle, is that the law (with rare exceptions) follows Hillel, and the second is that the law follows the majority. The system had flourished according to these guidelines for several centuries by the time this gemara was composed, and there is nothing "out there"—no historical reality—which requires that these principles be questioned. They could, by this point in rabbinic history, be applied comprehensively and without dissent. So, when the gemara questions the comprehensiveness of their application, it can be doing so only in the pursuit of theoretical possibilities. However theoretical, though, they are undeniably radical, allowing those who would translate these theories into practice to sidestep the most fundamental defining principles of the community. Moreover, as we see immediately following, this theory is not—in the present context, at least—divorced entirely from reality.

The opinions of Abbaye and Rava that follow (t through v) resolve the conflict between the prohibition of sectarianism and the opinion that the Shammaites actually followed their views by claiming that the prohibition "don't make factions" applies in only very limited circumstances. In Abbaye's answer, "don't make factions" pertains only to a single city; in different cities, though, different practices are permissible. Rava rightly objects, pointing out that the model of Hillel and Shammai is one in which different practices coexisted in the same city. Therefore, Rava suggests, the prohibition of "don't make factions" must apply only to a single court. Different courts, however, may legitimately issue different rulings even in a single city.

There is no doubt that Rava's opinion is the better resolution of the conflict at hand. Moreover, Rava's challenge to Abbaye is never responded to. Thus, at this stage, the more permissive interpretation seems to be preferred. Furthermore, given the gemara's introduction, the permissive consequences of Rava's interpretation (or, for that matter, Abbaye's) now pertain even to Shammaites who follow their opinions *after the heavenly voice in Yavne!* In the fourth century (the time of Abbaye and Rava) and beyond, if Shammaites wish to follow their opinions in practice, they may legitimately do so! Though perhaps originally more modest, in their present context the halakhic interpretations proposed by these amoraim (particularly Rava!) become tools of the broadest possible toleration.

The series of "objections" that follows (w forward) serves the same rhetorical purpose. To appreciate these steps, we must approach them with the question demanded of any reader here: Against which opinion are these objections directed? The tannaitic texts (baraitot) quoted in (w), with the clarifying voice of the gemara itself ("In R. Eliezer's place they would [do so, but] in R. Aqiba's place they would not"), seem to suggest that different practices may be supported in different locales but not in the same city. Thus, this might appear to be an objection against Rava and a support of Abbaye. But the next step (x) makes it clear that this would be a misinterpretation. When the gemara responds, saying, "What sort of objection is this? [We have already learned that, even according to the stricter interpretation of 'don't make factions,'] different places are different!" it becomes evident that the objection is directed *against* the opinion that restricts diversity in practice (that is, the opinion that the School of Shammai *did not act*—or, if you prefer, "don't make factions"). This might itself be surprising enough, but the fact that the objections are inadequate to the task—as the gemara itself admits [3]—is even more perplexing. The objections refer to cases in which different laws were practiced in different locations (hence the objection: "See! They *did* act on the basis of their opinions!"), but, following the interpretations of Abbaye and Rava, this would not represent a problem. Even according to Abbaye, there can be no objection to different practices in different towns. So what is the point?

The next objection (aa) fails on the same account. It observes that R. Abbahu would practice the Shabbat law differently in different places, thus apparently contradicting the prohibition against differing practices. But, again, by this point we already know that "different places are different," so the objection is itself a puzzling one. The gemara (cc through dd) resolves this problem by suggesting that the objection was never really directed against the "don't make factions" law. Its real object was the differing practices of the same person.

Rhetorically, these flawed objections accomplish two things. First, they illustrate prominent cases in which, even in matters as serious as shabbat and kashrut, a variety of practices were tolerated. Second, by pointing out that, in light of the interpretations of Abbaye and Rava, the opinion that demands "don't make factions" applies only (possibly) in the same town, the "restrictive" opinion turns out to be extremely tolerant. By means of the qualifying remarks of Abbaye and Rava, which the gemara, in these "objections," insists that we notice, the denial of legitimate alternatives in practice is far more restricted. The objections don't work precisely because the other party *already agrees* that alternatives should be supported.

It is only the last objection, referring to the mamzer problem (gg through jj), that grants the serious consequences of factionalism. The gemara at first seems to admit the severity of this problem, but by means of a simple suggestion even this is resolved, and its final opinion, like those that preceded, is permissive.

But, given the nature of the solution, this final objection, too, turns out to have been a poor one. For an objection to be effective it must be supported by convincing logic and it must not admit an obvious answer. Lack of logical support is the problem with the first two objections, as we noted. The final objection is undone by a failure to satisfy the second criterion. How is this "undoing" accomplished? Following a response to the second "objection" and immediately preceding the third, a seemingly irrelevant "rhetorical" question is asked concerning the servant of R. Abbahu (ee). How can R. Abbahu, the gemara wants to know, act in different ways in different places in a manner that is perfectly consistent with the halakha but might, nevertheless, lead his attendant to draw the wrong conclusion? The answer: "He *informed* his attendant [of the reasons for his actions]." However irrelevant the question might seem to be, the answer is perfectly reasonable, and the reader proceeds with the knowledge that apparently difficult halakhic quagmires can be overcome through clarification and the sharing of information. Therefore, when the gemara turns its attention to the difficulties created by the practice of differing marriage laws, the reader already knows a solution. When the gemara then suggests precisely this solution in response to the final objection (the two schools could act in accordance with their views because they *informed* one another of any problems), the reader responds, "Of course! This was never really a problem in the first place!" The gemara provided the solution before it raised the problem. At the very moment the mamzer objection is articulated, the response is already at hand. Far more than a mere "rhetorical question," then, the brief exchange concerning the servant served rhetorically to render even this single "good" objection ineffective.[4]

What is the point of parading these three objections before the reader's eyes, only to emphasize that there are no real objections at all? The first two objections are directed against the restrictive opinion. By highlighting the pointlessness of the objections, the gemara reminds us that there is no real restrictive opinion against which to object. As we said above, if the other party already agrees with you, what's the argument? In this case, what the other party already agrees with is the permissibility of practicing halakha according to different opinions, at least in different cities.

The third objection ostensibly seeks to demonstrate that Shammaites (and other factions) could not reasonably have acted on the basis of their opinions. Those who claim that they did act must therefore be wrong. But this conclusion would obviously be erroneous, for, as the gemara has earlier pointed out, the sharing of information can help overcome even the most serious such halakhic predicament. Here the gemara emphatically announces that there are no insurmountable problems with a pluralistic halakhic reality. Don't object to different practices. Factionalism is not factionalism at all.

The final steps of the sugya (ll through nn) affirm the correctness of the previous response ("they informed them"), thus also reconfirming that tolerance and trust is the appropriate response to even serious potential problems resulting from pluralistic practice. By declaring in conclusion that "this also makes sense"—a statement that is used sparingly enough to be noteworthy[5]—the gemara ensures that there will be no mistaking the thrust of its argument. This final emphatic repetition, the context established by the gemara, and the overall deliberation with its careful turns and manipulations all serve to create a surprisingly forceful statement on behalf of the legitimacy of different practices in different rabbinic communities. Given the care with which this argument was formulated, I have little doubt that the mind(s) behind the sugya recognized the message here communicated.

We see, then, that the Bavli's theory of theory also extends to its theory of practice. Though we would easily have understood a wisdom calling for limits on practical pluralism, this sugya did not demand this of us. Different masters interpret God's revealed will differently and we, who locate ourselves in the communities of different masters, have the right to live by our convictions. This is the social-halakhic program proposed by this text. It is a program that lived by its convictions—theoretical and practical—and generated a Judaism which was, throughout its history, remarkably diverse.

7.

Women
Categorized

The interplay between theory and practice is a subject of constant fascination in the Bavli. Some deliberations support a wide variety of theoretical approaches but do not suggest what consequences, if any, there might be in practice. Others, such as the sugya examined in chapter 6, are explicit in supporting the legitimacy of pluralistic practice. Still others, as we shall see, support the singular law of the Mishnah but let it be known that there are theoretical alternatives or near-alternatives. The rhetorical impact of the latter sort of deliberation, supporting decided law but revealing the theoretical multiplicity behind the singularity of the Mishnah, demands interpretation: Why uphold the Mishnah's law but diminish its theoretical support?

The texts examined in this chapter tackle two forms of Mishnaic law-writing—list-making and categorization. Both forms are central to the world-organizing project of the Mishnah and both are commonly subjected, in the gemara, to testing and critique. When the two forms overlap—that is, when the Mishnah's definition of a category allows one to evaluate a related list (and vice versa)—then analytical possibilities are particularly rich. What if the list merely reiterates in detail what the category definition would have led us to expect in any case? Why specify superfluously? On the other hand, what if the list and the category definition (the general rule) do not align? How do we explain the Mishnah's inconsistency? Each of these scenarios promises fruitful speculation in the gemara.

The subject of the two sugyot examined below is the halakhic status of women. In particular, these texts address the question of which (categories of) mitzvot women are or are not obligated to observe, and, in the second sugya, the basis of such obligations or exemptions. Though the sugyot mostly do not quote common sources, they clearly assume a common stock of principles. Together they serve to elaborate, in the fullest way in classical rabbinic literature, the position of women in the larger halakhic system.

We will first study the briefer of the two texts (Ber. 20b), a discussion of a variety of practices—perhaps meant to represent larger categories—that women, slaves, and minors are or are not obliged to perform. The Mishnah (3:3) states the law simply:

A. Women, slaves, and minors are exempt from the reading of the Shema and from tefillin

B. and are obligated in prayer (tefillah = the amidah), in the mezuzah and in birkhat hamazon [= the blessing for food eaten].

The Mishnah, typically, does not justify its law or explain the categories to which particular practices are assigned. At present, we have merely a list of practices which are or are not incumbent upon the sorts of people listed in (A). It will be up to the gemara's commentary to direct our attention to matters of principle and generalization.

The gemara, as printed, appears to address each of the details of the Mishnah bit by bit (my translation recreates the atomized quality of the printed text). However, if we consider the Talmudic deliberation more broadly, we will see that certain strategies unite the gemara's overall approach to the Mishnah:

I.

a. The reading of the Shema—this is obvious [and the Mishnah should have no need to tell us something obvious]!

b. [For] it is an affirmative time-bound commandment and women are exempt from all affirmative time-bound commandments (see m. Qid. 1:7)!

c. What might you have said [that would have led you to believe that this is an exception to the general rule, in which case the Mishnah would not be telling us something obvious]?

   d. Since it [the Shema] has in it the [acceptance of the yoke of the] kingdom of heaven [(see m. Ber. 2:2), which is so important that women should also be obligated to perform this commandment].

   e. [The law of the Mishnah] comes to teach us [that this is not so].

II.

   a. And from tefillin—this is obvious [since it, too, is an affirmative time-bound commandment].

   b. What might you have said [that would have led you to believe that this is an exception to the general rule]?

   c. Since it is equated [that is, juxtaposed, in scripture (see Deut. 6:8–9)] to mezuzah [for which women are obligated, for this too they should also be obligated].

   d. [The law of the Mishnah] comes to teach us [that this is not so].

III.

   a. And they are obligated in prayer—for they [prayers] are [petitions for] mercy.[1]

   b. What might you have said [that would have led you to the opposite conclusion, making this teaching of the Mishnah essential]?

   c. Since it is written "Evening, morning, and at noon [I pray and cry aloud]" (Ps. 55:18), it is like an affirmative time-bound commandment [from which women should be exempt].

   d. [The law of the Mishnah] comes to teach us [that this is not so].

IV.

   a. And in mezuzah—this is obvious [since it is not a time-bound commandment, why would we imagine otherwise?]!

   b. What might you have said [that would have led you to the opposite conclusion, making this teaching of the Mishnah essential]?

   c. Since it is equated [that is, juxtaposed, in scripture (see Deut. 11:19–20)] with the study of Torah [from which women are exempt, they should also therefore be exempt from it].

   d. [The law of the Mishnah] comes to teach us [that this is not so].

V.

   a. And in birkhat hamazon—it is obvious [since it is not an affirmative time-bound commandment].

   b. What might you have said [that would have led you to the opposite conclusion]?

c. Since it is written "when the Lord shall give you in the evening meat to eat and bread in the morning to be filled" (Exod. 16:8), it is like an affirmative time-bound commandment [from which women should be exempt].

d. [The law of the Mishnah] comes to teach us [that this is not so].

VI.

a. R. Ada b. Ahava said: Women are obligated in the sanctification of the day [kiddush for Shabbat] as a matter of Torah . . .

It is necessary, of course, to analyze each of the specific delibera-tions, but a quick review of this text will already permit us to make a couple of important observations: (1) Despite the fact that the Mishnah speaks of women in combination with slaves and minors, the gemara's concern is primarily the status of women in these matters (the Mish-nah in Qiddushin that states the general rule concerning affirma-tive time-bound commandments speaks of women, not of slaves and minors); (2) The text as a whole is an essay in what we might call near-exceptions, because the only way the laws enumerated in this Mishnah are not obvious (which, in the opinion of the gemara, would be unacceptable) is to claim that they might with good reason have been included in the opposite category. Each, therefore, is actu-ally an exception to the general rule or, at least, might easily have been.

Let us explore this second observation in greater detail. The first segment of the gemara (I.a) observes that the Mishnah seemingly teaches us something that should be obvious, that is, that women are exempted from the Shema, an affirmative time-bound command-ment. This should be obvious because the Mishnah elsewhere (Qid. 1:7) spells out the general rule that women are exempted from such obligations; if the specific (the Shema) is subsumed under the general (affirmative time-bound commandments) there is no need to elaborate the specific. Assuming that the Mishnah, like the Torah itself, will not repeat itself unnecessarily, the gemara views this apparent redun-dancy as a problem and is therefore compelled to argue that there is no actual redundancy at all. The Shema, the gemara proposes, might have been regarded as an exception to the Mishnah's general rule on account of its paramount importance. That is, by virtue of the ac-knowledged centrality of the Shema as both ritual and statement of creed, it would have been perfectly reasonable to conclude that women *should* be obligated to recite the Shema despite the general rule suggesting the contrary. So when the present Mishnah declares that women are exempt from reciting the Shema, it is telling us something that would not otherwise have been obvious, whatever some general ruling might have suggested. The gemara, in the end, upholds the law of the Mishnah, but one is nevertheless left with the impression (necessary for the logical consistency of this gemara!) that it could just as easily have rendered the contrary ruling.

The same approach is articulated in the second segment, but with potentially further-reaching consequences. In this instance, the gemara observes that the Mishnah's teaching exempting women from the commandment of tefillin (prayer straps) should be obvious (for the same reason as the Shema). To counter this problematic conclusion, the gemara proposes that tefillin might, by virtue of its scriptural proximity to mezuzah, have been equated with the latter. Since women are obligated to mark the doorposts of their homes (mezuzah), such an equation would have led us to consider women obligated in tefillin as well. To prevent this conclusion, the present Mishnah teaches that the law is the opposite. But, again, for this analysis to be logically sound, it is necessary for the position being rejected (that women are obligated in tefillin) to be reasonable; otherwise the Mishnah would be teaching something obvious (something that Torah—in this case, Oral Torah—may not do, according to the talmudic rabbis)! Yet this reasonable position injects an ironic and potentially subversive note into the deliberation, for, as is well known, the very justification offered by the gemara (see Qid. 34a, analyzed below) to support the general rule exempting women from affirmative time-bound commandments rests on the equation of all such commandments with tefillin. If tefillin itself might just as easily have been compared to mezuzah, thus rendering women obligated, then the very foundation of the general principle, as proposed in Qiddushin, falls away. There would be no general rule, then, and all we would be left with are individual rulings.

The next part of the gemara, discussing prayer (III), takes the category confusion already hinted at in the prior steps and blows it up to immense proportions. Perhaps for this reason, the printed text, as translated here, reflects emendations proposed by Rashi. The text Rashi had in front of him read as follows:

a. Prayer—it is obvious!
b. Since it is written "Evening and morning and at noon I speak and moan" (Ps. 55:18), it is like an affirmative time-bound commandment [and thus women should be exempt].
c. [Therefore the Mishnah] comes to teach us that it [prayer] is [begging for] mercy [and women are thus obligated].[2]

The problem with the more original text is obvious: In common experience, Jewish prayer is an affirmative time-bound commandment (its recitation is required at certain specified periods of the day). Not only is it not "obvious," therefore, that women should be obligated to recite prayer, but anyone equipped with knowledge of the rituals of prayer and the general rule would conclude quite the opposite—that women are exempt! Is it possible that, in reality, prayer is *not* time-bound? Perhaps the times for its recitation are not specific enough to place it in this category? Surely this conclusion would be suggested by step (b), which states that prayer is *"like* a . . . time-bound commandment" (but is not actually one). But if this were so, by what rationale is tefillin a time-bound commandment? Its obligation extends to the entirety of the day! In fact, for this very reason, there are noted Mishnaic authorities who believe that tefillin is not a time-bound commandment (on the consequences of this, see our analysis of the Qiddushin gemara, below in this chapter)! Any claim for the "obvious" in this context evaporates in confusion, and for this reason we understand Rashi's emendation, which eliminates the term "obvious" entirely.

But Rashi's reading, along with the unemended version, still emphasizes that prayer is an exception to the general rule. When the gemara (III.c) states that prayer is "like an affirmative time-bound commandment," we readily understand that it *is* just such a commandment. Thus, a woman's obligation in this ritual is contrary to the general rule. Why was this exception thought necessary? Because prayer is a petition for mercy, and even women need such petitions. The reasoned conclusion triumphs over the purely technical conclusion; whatever strict category analysis might have demanded, an open-eyed account of the human realities demands the opposite.

But, with this information in mind, we are invited to return to the previous section. There we learned that it might have been reasonable to obligate women in the recitation of the Shema because it constitutes "the acceptance of the yoke of the Kingdom of Heaven." We understood that this needed to be a reasonable possibility, but we also saw that the general rule was upheld, despite reason to conclude the contrary. Was this because general rules always triumph in the halakhic system? Now, we discover, the answer is no. Sometimes general rules yield to other wisdoms. Is there a good reason, then, that in the case of the Shema the general rule was not compromised whereas in the case of prayer it was? Apparently not.[3] If not, then why does the Mishnah suggest opposite conclusions? We have no answer to this question. All we know is that general categories are impossible to construct; on the contrary, reasoned analysis readily yields their deconstruction.

The next segment of the gemara (IV) similarly calls into question the validity of the general formulation of Mishnah Qiddushin, but now from the opposite direction. According to that Mishnah, women are obligated to perform affirmative commandments that are not tied to any specific time. It should therefore be obvious, as the gemara notes, that women are obligated to attach mezuzahs to the doorposts of their homes. Again, it is formally inadmissible (in the opinion of the gemara) for the Mishnah to teach something we could have known from elsewhere, so it argues—as we should already expect—that we might reasonably have concluded that mezuzah does not abide by the general rule. Because of this potential conclusion, the Mishnah was forced to record the present ruling.

In this case, the potential subversion of the general categories is accomplished on several fronts. First, as above, we discover that mezuzah could easily have been thought an exception to the general category. Will such exceptions always be turned back? From the information now at hand, we cannot know that this is so. Moreover, the reason for the potential exception—the possible equation with study of Torah—draws our attention to a bona fide exception. Torah study is not bound by time, yet women are exempt. Hence, the general rule is not without exceptions. Is there a good reason that Torah study is an exception and mezuzah not? At present, we don't know. All we know is that the general ruling need not triumph. Our confidence in that general instruction cannot, therefore, stand unweakened. Finally, the equation that is here turned away is apparently identical in kind to the equation that serves as the basis of exempting women from affirmative time-bound commandments. That equation, spelled out in the gemara in Qiddushin (and analyzed below), is derived from the scriptural juxtaposition of tefillin and the study of Torah. If the present equation with mezuzah need not be upheld, then why should the equation with tefillin? Indeed, the gemara in Qiddushin addresses precisely this question. But is the reader of this gemara assumed to know the answer there? And, in light of the current confusion of trends (some equations are upheld, some dismissed), will the reader be convinced by distant answers? At present, it is the exceptions and possible exceptions which emerge more clearly. Systemic coherence is not, apparently, the message of the current deliberation.

Lest these points be missed, the gemara goes on (VI) to explicitly discuss a matter (kiddush, the blessing of the Sabbath day over wine) that is obviously an exception to the general rule. The deliberation follows.

a. R. Ada b. Ahava said: Women are obligated in the sanctification of the day [kiddush for Shabbat] as a matter of Torah.

b. For what reason? It is an affirmative time-bound commandment and women are exempt from all affirmative time-bound commandments!

c. Abbaye said: [The obligation is actually] from the rabbis.

d. Rava said to him: He said "a matter of Torah" [and not from the rabbis].

e. And furthermore, [if the rabbis are going to obligate women to perform this affirmative time-bound commandment then] let us obligate them to perform all affirmative time-bound commandments on the authority of the rabbis!

f. Rather, Rava said: Scripture said "Remember" and "Observe" (Exod. 20:8 and Deut. 5:12) [these words serving as the first words of the Sabbath commandment in the two versions of the Ten Commandments]— [implying that] everyone who is included in [the obligation of] observing [not profaning the Sabbath; a negative commandment for which women are obligated] is included in [the obligation of] remembering [sanctification of the day].

g. And these women, since they are included in observing, they are [also] included in remembering [now as an obligation of the Torah].

As we continue through the gemara's purported commentary on the Mishnah, the first question we must ask is this: Why does the gemara now discuss kiddush, a ritual that finds no mention in the present

Mishnah? The obvious connection is the question of women's obligations, but this is not a sufficient explanation, for there are other rituals
that would on this basis likewise demand discussion here. Notably,
kiddush, like prayer, is an affirmative time-bound commandment for
which women are obligated, but so too is the obligation to eat matzah
on Passover, for which, according to rabbinic tradition, women are
similarly obligated. Moreover, unlike prayer, kiddush is clearly understood to be a commandment of the Torah. So something beyond the
obvious must explain the placement of the present discussion in this
particular context.

As we consider the give-and-take of the gemara's deliberation, it
becomes evident that the text is interested in emphasizing the exceptional quality of kiddush. The first question (b) objects to the teaching
that "women are obligated in the sanctification of the day as a matter
of Torah": How can women be obligated in this commandment if the
general rule would demand otherwise? The first answer (that of Abbaye) proposes that the obligation of women is actually merely rabbinic, assuming, obviously, that the general principle of Mishnah
Qiddushin describes only the Torah's system. But, even if this weren't
so obviously incorrect (as Rava emphatically points out), it is hardly
satisfactory. If the rabbis wish to go beyond what the Torah would
require of women in this case, why not do so in all cases (e)? Besides,
the initial teaching does say "as a matter of Torah," so it is hardly
worth exploring this proposed solution in any case.

What is the point of these several steps? Could Abbaye really have
said "from the rabbis" if the teaching before him said "as a matter of
Torah?" Or is not the point to insist that we are working here with
one system, not two, a system which is riddled with exceptions (or, if
you prefer, a system which will not be controlled by general rules)?
The Torah, the gemara in Qiddushin insists, exempts women from
affirmative time-bound obligations, except where it doesn't. And in
the case of kiddush, the gemara forcefully demonstrates, it doesn't. In
this matter, women *are* obligated—according to the Torah.

To show that the Torah's inconsistency is precisely the point, the
gemara goes on, in the final steps of this discussion (not quoted here),
to show that women are exempted by the Torah from reciting the
blessing after meals. By virtue of being categorized with minors in an
authoritative source, quoted in context, the gemara concludes that the
obligation of women could not possibly be from the Torah (minors do

not have bona fide obligations, according to the rabbis' understanding of the Torah). Yet the blessing after meals is not a time-bound commandment; it is the act of eating and being sated that creates the obligation, not the specific time of day. According to the same Mishnah in Qiddushin, women *are* obligated to perform such commandments, apparently according to the Torah. So here we have another exception, in this case in the opposite direction. There can be no doubt at this stage: exceptions, if they are not the rule, at least break the rule.

To return to the observation I made earlier: It is reasonable to characterize this sugya as an essay in exceptions and near-exceptions. The principle of Mishnah Qiddushin, telling us which commandments women are or are not required to perform, is subject to a most persistent challenge in this text. The specifics of the Mishnah are, in the end, upheld, but that is not what the gemara is "about." Nor is this, in any accepted sense of the term, a commentary on the Mishnah. All we ever learn in the gemara is why the law might have been other than it is. Never is the actual law of the Mishnah defended. Never is it justified by explicit reference to a source-text. If we are meant to assume that the Mishnah in Qiddushin justifies the present Mishnah's rulings, then it is odd that the gemara provides concrete examples of exceptions to that Mishnah's stated principle. What emerges most clearly is the vulnerable quality of category-boundaries construed on the basis of general principles. The reader does not conclude his or her study of this gemara with the confidence that he or she could predict the rule in any case not explicitly mentioned.

The gemara that deliberates upon the Mishnah in Qiddushin begins by making explicit what is only implied in the Berakhot text: We do not learn from general principles. This conclusion follows a list of exceptions to the general rule, suggesting that the broad purpose of the Qiddushin gemara is identical to its Berakhot counterpart as we have understood it. The first section of the sugya in Qiddushin ostensibly exemplifies the categories "time-bound" and "non–time-bound":

a. [Mishnah:] All affirmative time-bound commandments [men are obligated and women are exempted. And all affirmative commandments not bound by time, both men and women are obligated.]

b. Our sages taught: What is an affirmative time-bound commandment? [The obligation to erect a] sukkah and [the obligation to wave a] lulav and [the obligation to blow a] shofar and [the obligation to wear] fringes and tefillin [prayer-straps].

c. And what is an affirmative non–time-bound commandment? [The obligation to attach a] mezuzah [to the door-posts of your house] and [the obligation to erect a] railing [along the edge of your flat roof] and [the obligation to restore a] lost object [to its owner and the obligation to] send off a baby bird [when taking the mother].

d. And is this [truly] a general rule? But, behold, [the obligation to eat] matzah [on Passover] and [the obligation to engage in] rejoicing [on the festivals] and [the obligation of] gathering [with the rest of the people during the sabbatical year to hear the public reading of the Torah] are affirmative time-bound commandments, yet women are obligated [which, according to the general rule, they should not be].

e. And, moreover, the study of Torah and [the obligation to] be fruitful and multiply and [the obligation to] redeem the [first-born] son [from the priests], which are not affirmative time-bound commandments, yet women are exempted [though, according to the general rule, they should be obligated to perform such commandments]!

f. Rabbi Yoḥanan said: We do not learn from general rules, even in a place where it says "except [for]" [in which case we might think that, exceptions being specified, these are the only exceptions] . . .

At its beginning, this gemara seems to be a straightforward clarification of the terms used in the Mishnah (affirmative time-bound commandments, affirmative non–time-bound commandments). But, after having given illustrative examples of the said categories, the gemara immediately questions the integrity of the Mishnah's rule, providing specific and unchallenged examples that contradict it. The conclusion, supported with another example of the same phenomenon (in steps not quoted above), is that "We do not learn from general rules." Repeated twice and unquestioned in context, this conclusion stands as the definitive view of the gemara.

The next lengthy section goes on to seek the source of the Mishnah's rule ("All affirmative time-bound commandments, women are exempt"). But, with the context provided by the "introduction" just seen, it is an odd exploration indeed. The reader is forced to ask, "What is the value of the source of such a rule?" The rule by itself helps little, for we have already been put on notice that such rules admit for exceptions, and specific exceptions have already been enumerated. It would seem that we need additional information before we can know whether the rule applies or not. So what is the value of the rule, source or not? Perhaps, we will hope, the following deliberation will provide not only a source but also guidelines for application. But alas, as we shall see, the gemara only highlights new exceptions, adding no guidelines for the adjudication of unknown cases. Moreover, the way the biblical source of the Mishnah's rule is (or is not) uncovered further confounds our confidence in the rule and its systemic integrity.

The sugya following is, as we have said, very lengthy and extremely complicated. We will examine most, but not all, of the sugya at hand, stopping where necessary for clarification and analysis.

a. [Mishnah:] And affirmative time-bound commandments . . . women are exempt . . .
b. Where [do we know it] from?
c. Learn [it by analogy] from tefillin—just as [in the case of] tefillin women are exempt, so too all affirmative time-bound commandments women are exempt.
d. And tefillin, learn it from the study of Torah—just as [in the case of] the study of Torah women are exempt, so too [in the case of] tefillin women are exempt.

The first proposed source of the Mishnah's general rule employs tefillin to represent the entire category of commandments that resemble it (affirmative [you must do it] time-bound [it must be done at a particular time]). The gemara assumes that we admit the validity of such a method, and it assumes (for the moment) that we will assent to tefillin as a model for the entire category (as opposed to some other affirmative time-bound commandment—say, matzah, which, as we learned above, women are obliged to perform). But, of course, if the argument is not to be absolutely and fatally circular, we must then determine why women are exempt from tefillin, and the reason cannot be the rule we are trying to derive from this model case. The gemara proposes (d) that the exemption of women from tefillin may be derived from their exemption from the study of Torah (apparently because of the juxtaposition of these two commandments in scripture; see Deut. 6:7–8, 11:18–19) and, for the moment, this stands as the recognized source of the general rule.

But we, the readers, must ask some questions here. First, why is the preferred analogy to tefillin? The gemara anticipates this question, and proceeds, in the following steps, to answer it (see the following proof). Second, if the ultimate source of the exemption of women from affirmative *time-bound* commandments is the obligation to study Torah, then what do we do with our recognition that this obligation (henceforth: Talmud Torah) is a *non*–time-bound commandment?! Perhaps it would be better to use Talmud Torah as representative of its category and therefore exempt women from non–time-bound obligations. Wouldn't such a direct derivation be preferred to the two steps required for extending this conclusion to time-bound obligations? This question is *not* answered in context and it continues to nag as the sugya progresses. But other issues, and other difficulties, will soon demand our attention.

e. But let us [instead] compare tefillin to mezuzah [a commandment women are obligated to perform which is similarly juxtaposed to tefillin in scripture; see Deut. 6:8–9)!

f. Tefillin is equated with [juxtaposed to] Talmud Torah in both the first and second paragraphs [Deut. 6, 11; but] tefillin is not equated with mezuzah in the second paragraph [in which the obligation of Talmud Torah stands between tefillin and mezuzah; see 11:18–20].

For the moment, well and good. Two equations are reasonably preferred to one, so the gemara's present argument makes good sense. But not for long . . .

g. And let us compare mezuzah to Talmud Torah [thereby exempting women from the obligation of marking the doorposts of their homes with the designated scriptural portions] [because mezuzah and Talmud Torah are juxtaposed in Deut. 11—though *not* in Deut. 6]!

h. This should not enter your mind, for it is written [as a promise for fulfilling the commandment of mezuzah] "in order that your days be lengthened" (Deut. 11:21)—do men require life and women not require life?! [Obviously not! Therefore women must be addressed by the command to mark their doorposts.]

The very next step (g) suggests that a single juxtaposition may be sufficient to derive the kind of lesson suggested here, for Talmud Torah and mezuzah are juxtaposed in one but not both of the relevant scriptural paragraphs. Comparing the present step to what precedes, we now understand that the earlier response (f) merely suggests that two are better than one, not that one by itself is inadequate. But is this response convincing, or merely facile? If a single scriptural juxtaposition is admitted as potentially effective, why not admit this in the case of tefillin and mezuzah, particularly since Talmud Torah is anomalous for its category? Are two juxtapositions and anomaly *necessarily* preferred to one juxtaposition without anomaly? The questions mount.

Further confounding the argument is the refutation of the suggestion that mezuzah be equated with Talmud Torah (both are, after all, affirmative time-bound commandments!). This step (h) reads the promised reward of Deut. 11:21 as applying only to mezuzah, with which it is indeed juxtaposed. But according to what might be a preferred reading, the promise of reward extends to the performance of all the commandments delineated in this scriptural paragraph (the all-encompassing quality of the rewards and punishments described here is evident from the beginning of the paragraph) and the same argument would therefore apply to at least mezuzah, Talmud Torah, and tefillin. Moreover, the knowledgeable reader may easily find other promises of reward that extend to the Torah as a whole, and the question would therefore become, "Do men require divine grace and women not?" Maintaining the integrity of the decided law on the basis of scriptural sources begins to feel forced. The reader trained in talmudic method who applies this method will find her- or himself challenging the logic of the argument as it progresses. The cloth of the sugya frays at the edges and no one attempts to patch all the flaws.

At this point, the gemara goes on to challenge the (non-)controlling rule, using scripture itself to question its validity:

i. But, behold [the obligation to sit in a] sukkah, which is an affirmative time-bound commandment, as it is written, "You shall sit [or, better, "dwell"] in booths for seven days" (Lev. 23:42), yet the reason [that women are exempt] is that the Merciful One wrote [in the Torah, ibid.] "the citizen"—[understood by the rabbis] to exclude women. [The fact that the Torah needed to specify this exclusion means that] without this, women are obligated [suggesting that there can be no general rule]!

j. Abbaye said: It is necessary [for the Torah to write "the citizen" to teach us the exclusion of women, even despite the general rule, because] you might have thought to say, since it is written "You shall sit in booths"—you shall sit as you [normally] dwell; just as [normal] dwelling [involves] a man with his wife, so too [dwelling in the] sukkah [should involve] a man and his wife.

k. Rava said [34b]: It is necessary [because] you might have thought to say, learn it [by means of an equation, equating] the fifteenth [and] the fifteenth from the festival of matzot [Passover, which, like Sukkot, begins on the fifteenth day of the month]—just as there women are obligated, so too here women are obligated.

l. It is [therefore] necessary [for the Torah to write "the citizen" to teach us the exclusion of women, even despite the general rule].

The gemara notes (i) that the midrash derived the exclusion of women from the mitzvah of Sukkah from the Torah's term, "the citizen." Because of the gemara's common assumption that the Torah says nothing extraneous, this creates a problem. If there is a general rule excluding women from affirmative time-bound commandments, then the Torah shouldn't need to write "the citizen" to accomplish this in the case of sukkah (which is, after all, an affirmative time-bound commandment). The fact that this term was necessary implies, therefore, that the general rule was not the will of the Torah and its Author. This challenge is answered differently by two sages, which suggests that the problem is easily resolved, but at least one of those answers confounds as much as resolves the matter.

Abbaye's answer (j) suggests that, exceptionally, women might have been thought obligated to sit in the sukkah, since women are essential to normal "dwelling." The term "the citizen," it is claimed, comes to militate against this mistaken—but highly reasonable—conclusion. The term is thus explained and the general rule upheld. But the reader is unable to ignore the fact that, at least in the case of sukkah, the opposite conclusion would also have been reasonable. This near-exception is rejected, but so too is the necessary quality of the law as ultimately accepted.

Rabba's answer (k), on the other hand, draws the reader's attention to a bona fide exception. His solution suggests that since Sukkot and Passover begin on the fifteenth day of their respective months, an analogy might reasonably have been drawn between them. Hence, because women are obligated to eat matzah on Passover, they should similarly be obligated to sit in booths on Sukkot. Again, to militate against this possible conclusion, the Torah needed to write "the citizen," excluding women from the Sukkot obligation. Still, by upholding the general rule this way—by showing that, even assuming the general exemption of women, the Torah still had to record their exemption from Sukkot—Rava ironically highlights the fact that there *are* important exceptions to this very rule. If we defend a rule by noting possible and bona fide exceptions, have we genuinely constructed an effective defense? Or does a rule built on exceptions undermine itself from the very beginning?

The next brief sequence essentially recreates the exchange just examined. In this latter case, defense of the general rule requires our recognition that the exceptional obligation for women to hear, like men, the public reading of the Torah during the sabbatical year might easily have been extended to a related affirmative time-bound commandment. As in the preceding exchange, the general rule survives attack, but only after the reader's attention is drawn to the real exception.

In the following sequence, the Talmud brings to fruition the task begun earlier. This sequence is long and extremely complex, and it requires familiarity with several of the rabbis' most technical methods of interpretation. For present purposes, the following abbreviated version of the text will suffice.

1. And while we learn from [the model of] tefillin to exempt [women from affirmative time-bound commands] let us learn from [the model of] rejoicing [on the festival] to obligate [women]!

2. Abbaye said: A woman, her husband causes her to rejoice [and the obligation is actually his, not hers[4]] . . .

3. And let us learn from [the model of] gathering [to hear the Torah following the Sabbatical year, which women are obligated to do].

4. [We do not derive this conclusion] because matzah and gathering are two scriptures that come as one [or, teach the same thing; that is, both teach that women are obligated] and [the rule is that] any two scriptures that come as one, we do not teach [that is, we do not use them as the source of such derivations].

5. If so, tefillin and [the obligation] to be seen [at the Temple on the festival] are also two scriptures that come as one . . .

6. They are necessary [and therefore do not count as "two scriptures that come as one"] . . .

7. This is fine for the one who says we do not teach [such conclusions when there are "two scriptures that come as one"] but for the one who says we do teach, what is there to say?

8. And furthermore, [concerning] affirmative non–time-bound commandments, from where [do we know] that women are obligated?

9. It is learned from [the obligation to] fear [one's parents]—just as [in the case of] fear [of one's parents] women are obligated, so too [in] all affirmative non–time-bound commandments women are obligated.

10. And let us [instead] learn [the law of this category] from Talmud Torah [the obligation to study Torah, from which women are exempted]!

11. [We do not do this] because Talmud Torah and [the obligation to] be fruitful and multiply are two scriptures that come as one [both teach cases in which women are exempted from affirmative non–time-bound commandments] and [the rule is that] any two scriptures that come as one, we do not teach [that is, we do not use them as the source of such derivations].

12. [35a] And for R. Yoḥanan b. Beroka, who said [that] regarding both of them [Adam and Eve] he says, "and God blessed them, [saying] be fruitful and multiply" (Gen. 1:28), what is there to say [that is, why don't we exempt women from affirmative non–time-bound commandments on the basis of the model of Talmud Torah]?

13. Because Talmud Torah and redemption of the first-born [the obligation to redeem the first-born son from the priest] are two scriptures that come as one . . .

14. This is fine for the one who says we do not teach [such conclusions when there are "two scriptures that come as one"] but for the one who says we do teach, what is there to say? . . .

Even without all its details this is evidently an extremely complex exchange, demanding the highest level of concentration on the part of the reader and even then generating perplexity. It is reasonable, therefore, to ask whether this maelstrom of detail and counterdetail communicates a message. In addition, in the midst of this web the gemara once again emphasizes the scope of the exceptions, for every citation of "two scriptures that come as one" demands the availability of at least two exceptions to the general rule. Among exceptions to the rule exempting women from affirmative time-bound commandments are counted—in case we forgot—matzah and "gathering." Among exceptions to the rule obligating women to perform affirmative non–time-bound commandments are Talmud Torah, "being fruitful and multiplying," and redemption of the first born. As it did at the beginning, once again, as we approach the end, the gemara highlights the exceptions, confusing not only the categories but also the means by which these categories are derived. By now it is difficult not to despair of achieving clarity. Why does the gemara bring us, its students, to this point?

Another question: Having learned the other sugya (Berakhot) it is impossible for us not to wonder why *its* exceptions are not mentioned here. Prayer and kiddush are affirmative time-bound commandments, yet women are obligated. Blessing after meals is an affirmative non–time-bound commandment, yet women are (according to that sugya's understanding of the Torah) exempt. Are we meant to ignore these additional exemptions? Could the present gemara assume that we are not familiar with them? I think not (kiddush is too fundamental a ritual, and its status too often repeated, for us—advanced students of the rabbinic method—not to know it). In my reading, this gemara means to leave a "residue," a residue with important consequences. As we review this sugya's reasoning, we explicitly confront a number of important exceptions to the rules whose sources it seeks. But as these exceptions announce themselves, it is difficult for us not to recall that there are other exceptions which do not assert themselves so forcefully. They stand off in the wings. However, their presence is felt, and this implied presence prohibits us from comforting ourselves by saying, "Fine, so there are exceptions; but at least the exceptions are limited to those enumerated in context." This is, after all, not so; there are still more exceptions, more than the sugya can enumerate in context. If the borders of the categories are indistinct, so too are the borders of the sugya. Again, our desire for clearness of place is confounded. We cannot but be dissatisfied.

To respond to our dissatisfaction (which the gemara indeed anticipates), the text finally takes an entirely different tack, proposing a new derivation for the Mishnah's general rule.

aa. Rava said: The Paphunians know the reason for this thing [the rule excluding women from affirmative time-bound commandments],

bb. and who is it [that is, who is referred to by Rava]? R. Aḥa b. Yaakov [who said]: Scripture said, "and it shall be a sign on your hand and a memorial between your eyes, in order that the Torah of the Lord be in your mouth" (Exod. 13:9)—[In this verse] the *entire* Torah was equated with tefillin [which are the "sign" and "memorial"]; just as tefillin is an affirmative time-bound commandment and women are exempt, so too [with] *all* affirmative time-bound commandments women are exempt.

cc. And since women are exempt from affirmative time-bound commandments, it follows that women are obligated in affirmative non–time-bound commandments.

dd. This is well for the one who says that tefillin is an affirmative time-bound commandment, but for the one who says that *tefillin is an affirmative non–time-bound commandment,** what is there to say [to prove the Mishnah's general rule]?

ee. *Who is the one of whom you have heard that he said tefillin is an affirmative non–time-bound commandment?* R. Meir. And

---

* Emphases added; emphasized sections relate to discussion below.

he is of the opinion that [if there is a case of] two scriptures that come as one . . . we do not teach.

ff. And for R. *Judah* who said two scriptures that come as one we do teach and [he is also of the opinion that] *tefillin is an affirmative non–time-bound commandment*, what is there to say?

gg. Because matzah, *rejoicing*, and "gathering" are three scriptures that come as one [all teaching that women are obligated to perform an affirmative time-bound commandment] and [in cases of] three scriptures that come as one we do not teach [and we may therefore not teach, based upon these models, that women are obligated to perform affirmative time-bound commandments. Presumably, the operative model would therefore be the obligation to appear at the Temple on festivals, which is an affirmative time-bound commandment from which women are exempted].

This, the final section of this lengthy and remarkable sugya, is a denouement is the most literal sense: the entire fabric woven above unravels and we, the partners in that weaving, are left exhausted, not fully sure of where to go. Not only does the gemara now approach the question of the source of the Mishnah's general rule from an entirely different direction, it simultaneously undermines the very foundation upon which the earlier explanation was built. We are left stunned. Why, if a different path was necessary, was the first journey so long? But I am ahead of myself; first, let us attend to the details.

The proposed source of women's exemption from affirmative time-bound commandments seems to be simple enough. Exodus 13:9 speaks of "the entire Torah"[5] in combination with its specification of the tefillin commandment. This is taken to imply an equation of the entire Torah with tefillin: what is true of tefillin must also be true of Torah. Thus, if women are exempt from tefillin then women must similarly be exempt from. . . .

Herein lies the problem. Given the first midrashic statement of R. Aḥa b. Yaakov—"the entire Torah was equated with tefillin"—we would expect a statement of this sort to follow: "Just as tefillin, women are exempt, so too the entire Torah, women are exempt." In fact, I think it fair to say that an experienced student of rabbinic midrash will naturally fill in such a statement even before the gemara does so (I can attest that this is precisely what I did as I studied this sugya for the first time). Therefore, when the gemara suggests instead, "Just as tefillin is an affirmative time-bound commandment and women are exempt so too all affirmative time-bound commandments women are exempt"—adding "affirmative time-bound commandment" when neither the verse nor the initial midrashic derivation suggests it—the reader/student is thrown off balance. He or she says, "Wait; I thought it was the *entire* Torah which was being compared to tefillin, not just affirmative time-bound commandments!" Of course, this would be an unacceptable conclusion, because if the entire Torah were equated with tefillin, this would exempt women from the entire Torah (!). But the midrash is built on a misstep, and it is difficult to ignore that misstep. One cannot help but feel that the stated conclusion is forced—all the more so because the reader has long since known that what the midrash now says is incorrect. It is simply wrong to say (in language virtually identical with the Mishnah) "[for] *all* affirmative time-bound commandments women are exempt." We know well that this is not true of all affirmative time-bound commandments. The gemara undermines itself, and it is incumbent upon us to ask why.

If the deliberation ended here (at bb through cc), our problems would be large enough. But the continuation makes our difficulties even more severe. At (dd) we learn that not all sages are of the opinion that tefillin is a time-bound commandment. In the next two steps (ee through ff) we learn that both R. Meir and R. Judah are responsible for this contrary opinion. We take note; R. Meir and R. Judah are not insignificant figures. On the contrary, they are reasonably described as the two greatest sages of their mishnaic generation. Amoraic tradition has it (as the reader would well know) that unattributed Mishnahs are the opinion of Rabbi Meir, and the Talmud elsewhere speaks of him explicitly as the most brilliant sage of his time (Eruvin 13b, as we have seen in chapter 5). R. Judah is the most common disputant of R. Meir, and he too stands out as one of the luminaries of his generation. Thus, if both R. Meir and R. Judah are of the opinion that tefillin is not time-bound, it hardly matters who disagrees. This is a legitimate and even prominent opinion. Of course, if this opinion is true (as one of two "truths"), then the first lengthy deliberation—which stands on the analogy of all time-bound commandments with tefillin, likewise assumed to be a time-bound commandment—falls apart. So too, needless to say, does the midrash proposed at (bb). Shockingly, what we have assumed to be a given from the very first steps of the sugya now turns out to be anything but given. Again, as readers, we find solid ground melting beneath us.

Where are we at this stage? Is tefillin a time-bound commandment or is it not? If it is not, then are women obligated to perform it or not? The earliest scriptural equation would suggest that women are exempt from tefillin, whatever its time status. Are we to conclude, therefore, that women are exempt from this non–time-bound commandment, even though women are presumably obligated to perform other non–time-bound commandments, as a function of the general rule? Or will this new reality lead us in a new direction entirely? If we know that women are exempt from the non–time-bound commandment called tefillin, why do we not build the category, by analogy, on its basis, thus exempting women from all affirmative non–time-bound commandments? And why don't we then say, in the fashion of step (cc), "And since women are exempt from affirmative non–time-bound commandments, it follows that women are obligated in affirmative time-bound commandments"? All of these questions merely follow the lead of methods and logics the gemara already models. Why are these directions less legitimate than the ones it chooses?

In the end, the only thing everyone in the gemara may agree on is that the Mishnah is right—women *are* exempted from affirmative time-bound commandments. Otherwise, it is difficult to find agreement on fundamental issues at all. Some think tefillin is time-bound, others that it is non–time-bound. Some think we may learn when "two scriptures come as one," others think we may not. What is the meaning of this disagreement? What is the meaning of the confusing web in which these disagreements are represented?

At least, we might say, there is agreement on one matter of major consequence (the exemption of women). But is this really so? The gemara has listed several significant exceptions to the Mishnah's rule, and others not mentioned by this gemara are well known. Why the attention to the exceptions? Why does defense of the rule seem to depend so heavily on those exceptions?

Like the exceptions, the questions multiply, and they cannot be forgotten even though the sugya has come to an end. Notably, this sugya, like the one from Berakhot examined earlier in this chapter, leaves one with a powerful sense of what might have been—with a sense that contrary conclusions were not distant and, in significant cases, contrary conclusions were in fact realized. Why would these two related sugyas communicate this sense? Why do they render what might have been "natural" conventional, and what might have been neat (as a category) messy? We may only surmise.

Perhaps the gemara wishes to reveal to us—to readers as insiders—that the system upon which it deliberates does not always flow naturally or necessarily from its stated source, the Torah. I have argued that this is the lesson of other sugyas (see chapters 3 through 4), and it seems reasonable here as well. Why, in the company of insiders, would the rabbinic masters want this to be known? Perhaps to assert the power of the rabbinic Torah itself: the Mishnah's ruling *will* be upheld, whether the Written Torah requires it or not. Or perhaps the gemara wishes to record for posterity rabbinic countervoices, voices which doubt that the Mishnah elaborates the proper role of women in Jewish observance. Ambivalence and ambiguity—these are terms that for this reader correctly describe these sugyot which make their primary concern the status of women in Jewish society. Given the traditional "otherness" of women in rabbinic Jewish society, it seems to me that ambivalence and ambiguity are meaningful postures. Perhaps these gemaras hint at a turn to other values and opinions?

8.

The Problem with Foreskin: Circumcision, Gender, Impurity, and Death

A category is a complex construct. As observed in contemporary critical theory, it is defined as much by what it is not as by what it is.[1] Some elements of a category are more representative of/more central to the category than others.[2] Its boundaries are often indistinct. The community in which the category is meaningful changes and, with it, so do definitions and interpretations.

Sensitivity to each of these factors is evident in the Bavli's exploration of the category "Jewish male." The definition of this category is, I will argue, the concern of the first sugya in the eighth chapter of tractate Yevamot (70a and following). It begins, as we shall see, by focusing on the "other," that is, "the uncircumcised." By probing the symbolic and practical valences of "the uncircumcised," by suggesting or reinforcing associations of "the uncircumcised" with other "others," by seeking to understand the essence of the disqualification of "the uncircumcised," the Talmud reflects back upon the meaning of "the circumcised"—the Jewish male, as symbolized by the mark in his flesh.

My reading in this chapter focuses more on broad structures and intimated relationships than on all details of a single, contiguous text. This reading will be critical but not comprehensive, extensive but not complete. Before us we will find what appears a "typical" talmudic sugya, one which seems the product of associative accumulation.

However, with the insight of slightly different lenses, we will come to see it instead as a carefully crafted essay in categorization.

The sugya announces its concern with the first word of the Mishnah: "The uncircumcised." The question to be addressed, the Mishnah immediately makes clear, is the nature of the disability or disqualification constituted by the presence of a foreskin on a Jewish male; the uncircumcised man is equated with "all those who are [ritually] impure" and both categories of persons, we are told, are (in the event they are priests) ineligible to eat from terumah (obligatory gifts to the priests of grain, produce and livestock). The Mishnah, typically, doesn't explain either exclusion (though the reason for the exclusion of "those who are impure" will be known to any Jew who heard the reading of the Torah). What stands out at this first stage is the fact that men with a foreskin and impure individuals are grouped together at all. Why? What is the meaning of this implied association/equation?

Before progressing to the gemara, it is necessary to recall the biblical symbolism of circumcision and, briefly, the subsequent history of this mark in the flesh. It will readily be recalled that circumcision was the sign of the covenant that God commanded Abraham and his offspring to observe for all generations (see Genesis 17). By this mark, Abraham's stock would presumably be distinguished from all surrounding peoples. And, though other peoples in the Near East also practiced circumcision, subsequent to the triumph of Hellenism and its tastes (which considered circumcision mutilation), Jews were the last to hold on to this practice, one might say, "religiously." By the time of the composition of the Mishnah, both Jews and non-Jews saw the removal of the foreskin as *the* distinguishing mark of the Jewish male. Thus, for both biblical and historical reasons, circumcision marked the categories "inside" and "outside," who was a Jewish male and who not. No discussion of Jewish (male) identity could ignore this marker. No discussion of the presence or absence of foreskin could be divorced from basic issues of identity. This was a powerful sign with powerful symbolisms. The question was, simply, what precisely *were* its symbolisms? Or, to put it in a slightly different way, what *is* the problem with foreskin?

The gemara begins by asking the source of the Mishnah's disqualification of the uncircumcised priest from eating terumah:

a. It is taught [in a baraita]:

b. R. Eleazar[3] said: From where [do we know] that an uncircumcised male [priest] doesn't eat terumah?

c. It says "resident [alien] and hired slave" in [connection with] *pesah* (Exod. 12:45) and it says "resident [alien] . . . and hired slave" in [connection with] terumah (Lev. 22:10); just as "the resident alien and hired slave" mentioned in [connection with] *pesah*, the uncircumcised male is prohibited in its regard [see Exod. 12:48], so too "the resident alien and hired slave" mentioned in [connection with] terumah, the uncircumcised male is prohibited in its regard [by virtue of the equation implied by the common use of these terms in the two contexts].

d. R. Aqiba says: [this equation] in not necessary, for behold, He [God] says "A man, a man [from the seed of Aaron, *and he be leprous or experience a venereal flow*, he should not eat of the holy things . . .[4]]" (Lev. 22:4; emphasis added)—[this is meant] to include the uncircumcised male.

The first of the proposed proofs (b through c) roots the law of the Mishnah in scripture by means of an equation of scriptural phrases (a *gezeira shava*). On one level, this proof is an equation wherein the words or phrases upon which the equation is constructed serve as a kind of algebra: A = C and B = C; therefore A = B. In such an equation, C (that is, the common word or phrase) need not have any meaning relevant to the categories being equated (A and B). But, in this case, it is not impossible—indeed, as our analysis proceeds, it will in retrospect appear likely—that the nexus of this equation casts meaning on the equated categories. What distinguishes the resident alien and the hired servant is that neither is an Israelite and neither is circumcised. Neither, therefore, may partake of either the *pesah* sacrifice or of terumah. Here, we learn, the uncircumcised Jewish male may also partake of neither. But how complete is this proposed equation? To what extent, in other words, is the uncircumcised Jew like the resident alien or the hired servant? Is there some way that the uncircumcised Israelite male is *less* than an complete Jew?

The proof attributed to R. Aqiba (d) suggests another association. According to the version of our printed texts, the proof is based upon the repetition of the word "a man" (*"ish"*); the second "a man" is apparently understood to include that which is not stated explicitly—that is, the uncircumcised—in the law of the verse. But quotations of prooftexts in the Talmud (as in other rabbinic texts) are not precise, and it is not uncommon to find proofs built upon parts of verses which are not actually quoted. Moreover, as quoted in Rashi, the gemara includes the greater portion of the verse which serves as a prooftext (as included in brackets).[5] Thus, it may reasonably be assumed that the proof is built not only upon the repetition of "a man" but upon the repetition as it expands the meaning of the rest of the verse.

How, then, does the verse "prove" what R. Aqiba claims for it? The verse states that a priest ("a man from the seed of Aaron") who is leprous, or impure as a consequence of a venereal flow, should not eat "the holy," that is (for present purposes), terumah. The "problem" the text seeks to solve is the repetition of the word "a man." Why the repetition? The answer is that the Author (God) who repeats this term intends to include in the present law another category of persons, one not mentioned explicitly. But which category? What is the sense of including "the uncircumcised?" The answer must be the conceptual proximity of that which is understood to be implied (the uncircumcised) with that which is specified (the leper and the venereally impure). By saying the latter, and implying the inclusion of more than these, the verse (as understood by R. Aqiba) leads one to the uncircumcised through "natural" association. Suggesting in other terms what has already been implied in the Mishnah, the gemara says the Jewish male with a foreskin is like one impure. Moreover, the impurities with which the uncircumcised are associated are not minor. The leper must be expelled from the camp of Israel (Num. 5:2) and the one who has a flow must count seven "clean" days, immerse, and bring a sacrifice (Lev. 15:13–15) before he returns to a state of purity. These are severe disabilities, separating (to a greater or lesser degree) the afflicted individual from the company of other Jews. Does the present text imply that the uncircumcised male is similarly separated? To the present reader, it seems likely.

The gemara continues by testing R. Eleazar's proposed scriptural equation (b through c). After having determined that the equation stands upon firm ground, the gemara goes on (at 70b) to ask why *pesaḥ* and terumah should be equated for purposes of excluding the uncircumcised male. Granted that scripture signals some sort of equation, why should the uncircumcised be preferred to, say, the person who has lost a loved one, who is similarly disqualified from consuming the paschal lamb? The details of this line of questioning follow.

e. If so [that is, if there is indeed an equation to be made, perhaps it would be preferable to say:] what if [with regard to] a paschal sacrifice, an *onen* [one whose close relative has died but has not yet been buried] is prohibited [from eating] of it, so too terumah an *onen* is prohibited [from eating] of it.

f. R. Yose b. Ḥanina said: Scripture said "and every stranger [should not eat the holy]" (Lev. 22:10)—I [God] said to you strangeness and not the state of being an *onen*.

g. I could say [strangeness] but not the state of being uncircumcised!

h. But is it not written "resident stranger and hired servant" [in connection with both terumah and *pesaḥ*, which demands some sort of equation, as seen earlier]?!

i. And what did you see [which led you to prefer the inclusion of one and not the other on the basis of the scriptural equation]?

j. It makes sense that he should include the lack of circumcision [on the basis of this equation] for [one who is not circumcised] is lacking a [commanded] deed and the deed is in his body and his punishment is *karet* [excision, or being cut off from the soul of the people] and it applied even before [the revelation of] the word [at Sinai] and [the absence of] the circumcision of his male [children] and his slaves prevents [him from partaking of the paschal sacrifice].

k. On the contrary! He should have included the state of being an *onen* [on the basis of the scriptural equation] for it applies [potentially] at any hour [whereas the commandment to circumcise, once performed, no longer applies] and it is in practice for both men and women and he is not able to fix himself [unlike the uncircumcised state, which can be eliminated at his will].

l. These [the problems with uncircumcision] are more numerous [and therefore it makes more sense to exclude it on the basis of the equation] . . .

This stage of the deliberation represents an exercise in the explicit comparison and contrast of the state of uncircumcision and the state of being an *onen*. The problem that demands this comparison is that either could theoretically have been disqualified by the scriptural equation of *pesaḥ* and terumah. Our question must be "Why?" Why this comparison as opposed to some other?

To appreciate this exercise, it is necessary to consider what makes a comparison meaningful. It would be absurd—though by no means impossible—to compare, say, trucks and basketballs. The differences between the two are so extreme, and what they bear in common so insignificant, that listing such differences adds little to what is already obvious. For a comparison to be meaningful, it is necessary for the items compared to be sufficiently alike that highlighting their differences adds to what we already know. Ironically, this is both the power and the flaw of the common challenge, "You are comparing apples and oranges." As typically employed, this saying suggests that a person is comparing two items which are not sufficiently alike to make the comparison meaningful. It says, "What is the point of comparing these two things? They are so obviously different that your explicit comparison is silly." But the fact is that apples and oranges are sufficiently similar in common experience that a comparison of the two is indeed reasonable. Both are fruits, both are round, both produce juice, both have pits, and so on. So how are they different? Well, they have a different taste, one is orange when ripe, the other green or red, they have different vitamins, and so forth. Still, if one can say regarding two things that are so similar "you are comparing apples and oranges" (meaning, you are comparing things that are obviously different), then how similar must things be for sensible comparison? Similar indeed.

I begin with this analysis because, at first blush, the state of being uncircumcised and the state of being an *onen* seem to have nothing to do with one another. As the gemara itself points out when contrasting them, one is in the body, the other not; one applies to males and females, the other only to males; one entails one of the most severe of biblical punishments, whereas punishment is irrelevant to the other; and so on. So why does discussion of one lead to discussion of the other? What about the two causes us to associate them and demands that their differences be counted?

In other words, is there something about the foreskin that causes us (or should cause us) to think of death and mourning? Most explicitly, the Mishnah declares, in a tradition attributed to the School of Hillel, that "one who separates from the foreskin as though separates from the grave" (m. Pes. 8:8). The Mishnah speaks of a convert who converted immediately before Passover, so this teaching may perhaps be understood as a commentary on the idolatry from which the convert now separates: "Strange worship" *(avodah zarah)* is equated with death; worship of the true God brings life. Thus, when a man converts from a pagan religion to Judaism—separating from his foreskin in the process—it is as though he separates from the grave. This association of foreskin and foreignness is supported in the present gemara when, at (f), the state of being an *onen* is claimed to be excluded by the biblical reference to "strangeness," implying that the state of being uncircumcised *is not* immediately excluded by such a reference. True, the next step suggests that lack of circumcision might also be excluded. But this means only that the association is imperfect, not that there is no association at all between the two.

The conceptual relationship between foreskin and death must go deeper than this association to "strange worship," though, for the present teaching speaks not of a convert who separates from his foreskin, but of "the one who separates"—including, presumably, a Jew. Moreover, the gemara (Pes. 92a), in a tradition that has puzzled commentators, traditional and modern, declares that a Jew who, not having been circumcised as an infant, removes his foreskin must immerse in a ritual bath. For what reason? Though the gemara doesn't explain, the reason seems clear: the foreskin, the Mishnah teaches, is associated with the impurity of death. One who separates from death, being impure, must immerse.[6]

But, though understanding that the association is a general one, we have as yet come no closer to explaining it. What is it about the foreskin *as such* that suggests an association to death? In part, the proposed equation may be a reminder of the punishment for failure to circumcise—excision *(karet)*, sometimes called "spiritual death." Still, I would go a step further and argue that the absence of the basic covenantal symbol, the divine commandment to Abraham and his male offspring, is here thought to be death-like. The foreskin, like death, makes the male who has one *as though* impure (as we saw earlier) because it symbolically places him outside of the life of the covenantal community.

A cluster of common symbolisms begins to suggest a commentary on the meaning of uncircumcision. By building this cluster, the Talmud elaborates its commentary on the dangers of foreskin. Its commentary does not end here.

In the next several steps, the gemara quotes two biblical verses that limit the classes of persons who may legitimately partake of the paschal lamb. The first, Exodus 12:48, declares "any uncircumcised [male] may not eat of it," and the second, Exodus 12:43, states that "any foreigner may not eat of it." The gemara (at 71a) responds to the implied question "Why does the Torah have to teach both of these exclusions?" by explaining why it was necessary to teach both—that is, why one could not have been derived from the other. The explanation is this:

a. And it was necessary [for God, in the Torah,] to write "the uncircumcised" and it was necessary to write "the foreigner,"
b. for if the Merciful One [God] had written the uncircumcised [male, one might have thought that the reason for this exclusion is] because it is repulsive, but a [circumcised] foreigner, who is not repulsive, I might say no [he is not excluded from eating the pesah].
c. And if the Merciful One had written the foreigner [one might have thought that the reason for this exclusion is] because his heart is not [directed] to heaven, but the uncircumcised [Jew] whose heart is [directed] to heaven, I would say no [he is not excluded].
d. [Therefore] it was necessary [for God to write both exclusions in the Torah.

Again, we see the association of uncircumcision with foreignness. The implied question is, when one speaks of one, why doesn't the other naturally follow? True, the point of this exercise is to highlight the differences between the two. But let us again remember "apples and oranges." If the differences were too immediately obvious, then the comparison would be absurd, as would be the implied question. If only by contextual juxtaposition—here a quite pointedly scriptural juxtaposition—uncircumcision and foreignness are once more related.

But the more important contribution of the present exchange is its willingness, for the first time in this sugya, to explicitly address the question, "What is the problem with foreskin?" Its answer: it is repulsive, disgusting, vile (Aramaic: *ma'is*). In direct, even belligerent contradiction to the opinion of the surrounding Hellenistic culture which believed circumcision to be mutilation, the rabbinic view declares that the foreskin itself is repugnant. It is a blemish, a physical imperfection so hated by God that its bearer may not participate in the great meal of communal liberation.

But is it possible that *this* is the problem with foreskin? Is it the mere physical presence and appearance of this superfluous flesh that causes God to hate it so? After returning briefly to discuss R. Aqiba's opinion quoted at the beginning of this sugya, the gemara addresses just this matter, framing a question that brilliantly allows us to distinguish precisely what is and what is not the problem with foreskin.

a. R. Hama b. Uqba asked: An uncircumcised minor [before the eighth day following his birth], what is it [is it permissible] to anoint him with oil that is terumah?

b. Uncircumcision not in its time [that is, before the obligation to circumcise the baby obtains] does it disqualify or does it not disqualify?

How astute to frame the question this way! Before the eighth day of a Jewish boy's life, there is no obligation to circumcise him. Thus, during these few days following birth, the presence of the foreskin is not evidence of failure to uphold God's commandments, failure to bring the baby boy into the covenant of Abraham. If the child may nevertheless not derive benefit from terumah, then the problem must be foreskin *as such*. If the answer to R. Hama's question is "no," then something about the foreskin—its appearance, its presumed imperfection—must be so objectionable, so polluting, that even the newborn infant who has it must be disqualified. If, on the other hand, a baby with a foreskin may, before the eighth day of his life, derive benefit from terumah, then the problem would be the failure to perform the commandment. After the eighth day, the foreskin would therefore disqualify its bearer. Before the eighth day, no such disqualification would apply.

c. R. Zeira said: Come and hear [evidence which might suggest an answer]—I only know [from the verses at hand that] the [absence of] circumcision of his males at the time of doing [slaughtering the paschal sacrifice] and his servants at the time of eating [disqualifies him, the master of the household, from eating as well; see Exod. 12:48 for the former and 12:44 for the latter];

d. From where [that is, from what source] may I apply what is said [in connection] with this to that and what is said [in connection] with that to this?

e. Scripture says, "then" "then" [in both verses 44 and 48] for [purposes of constructing] a scriptural equation [a *gezeira shava*].

f. It is well [to say this concerning] his slaves [for] you will find that there are [that is, there could be] such [slaves] at the time of eating and not [yet] at the time of sacrifice—such as when they were purchased in between [the two events],

g. but his males [sons], how would you find them at the time of eating and not at the time of sacrifice? [Are we] not [therefore speaking of a case in which] he was born between the sacrifice and the eating?

h. [And would we not] learn from it [that is, from the fact that such an infant is here disqualified—and disqualifies his father—from eating the *pesah* that] uncircumcision before its time is [nevertheless counted as] uncircumcision?

i. Rava said: And figure it—"Let all his males be circumcised," said the Merciful One, "and then let him come forward to perform it" (Exod. 12:48); yet this one [the newborn infant] is not obligated to be circumcised!

j. Rather, what are we dealing with here [in the baraita quoted by R. Zeira, at c through e above]? Such as where a fever left him [between the sacrifice and the time for eating, making it possible for the first time to circumcise him during this period] . . .

Though involving several complex steps of analysis (many readers, I suspect, will fail to understand the details of the deliberation just quoted), the essentials of what is suggested here are actually quite straightforward: Following the question enunciated above—Is it the foreskin that matters, or the mitzvah?—the present steps first propose that it is the foreskin itself (h). How else could we imagine a case of "his male" (his son) who is uncircumcised at the time of the eating but not yet at the time of the sacrifice itself? Surely we must be speaking of a son born between the two events and, seeing that such a son disqualifies his father from eating the lamb (according to the present working interpretation), this must mean that the possession of a foreskin is by itself objectionable, even before the obligation to remove it applies. In the end (j and beyond) the gemara rejects this interpretation, insisting that there are alternative understandings of the case here discussed and that the true problem is the failure to circumcise when obligated. But the possibility that the problem lies with the foreskin itself has at least been entertained (meaning that it was not obviously unreasonable) and, as we shall see shortly, even when circumcision has been performed, the appearance of a foreskin is deemed highly objectionable. To be sure, the failure to observe God's command, as evidenced by the foreskin, is the primary concern. But the symbolic danger of the foreskin extends beyond this concern as well.

Undoubtedly, the primary association of the foreskin, beginning with the Mishnah and extending to several of the gemara's deliberations, has been with impurity, with secondary associations with death. These symbolic equations are proposed again at 71b, where R. Yoḥanan, in the name of R. Banaʾah, responds to the implied question: Does the "impurity" of the foreskin prevent one from eliminating other impurities? To appreciate the implied equation, we need review only the beginning of a segment that ultimately goes in other directions.

a. R. Yoḥanan said in the name of R. Banaʾah: An uncircumcised male may receive sprinkling [of the special waters to remove impurity after contact with the dead],

b. for we find that our ancestors received sprinkling when they were uncircumcised,

c. as it says, "and the people came up out of the Jordan on the tenth of the first month" (Joshua 4:19)—on the tenth they were not [yet] circumcised [see Josh. 5:2–3] because of the weakness [they experienced on account of the journey] of the road [through Sinai],

d. [and] the sprinkling [to purify them for the *pesaḥ*] when was it done to them? Was it not when they were uncircumcised? [The first of two required sprinklings over the course of a week had to occur before the tenth; otherwise they would not have been pure for the *pesaḥ* on the fourteenth of the month] . . .

On its face, the presenting question here is a strange one. As one medieval rabbinic commentator remarks, why *shouldn't* an impure (or uncircumcised) person be sprinkled? Even a woman impure by virtue of her menstruation may be sprinkled to remove the impurity of the dead![7] To make sense of the gemara's statement, therefore, we must assume that it would be reasonable to believe that the "impurity" of uncircumcision is sufficiently powerful to prevent the removal of other impurities. Furthermore, the "impurity" of uncircumcision must be, in some manner, comparable to or related to the impurity of the dead, for it is just this impurity its removal might prevent. To be sure, the teaching attributed to the named sages declares that purification may nevertheless take place. But the opinion is directed against another one—an opinion which is reasonable enough to demand response. As we have seen, this other opinion is the one which believes the impurity of uncircumcision to be (nearly) as powerful as the impurity of the dead. In the end, we learn, this belief is mistaken—but not so mistaken that it can be dismissed without comment.

From this point, the gemara goes on to explore the surprising and troubling reality just touched upon—the failure of the children of Israel in the desert of Sinai to circumcise their sons. Following this related discussion, the gemara (at 72a) returns to the question so often addressed above (what is the problem with foreskin?), now addressing it from a slightly different perspective. Again, only a few steps of the deliberation are necessary to appreciate its contribution to the larger discussion:

   a. R. Huna said: As a matter of Torah, a man the skin of whose penis has been pulled forward [to make it appear that he has a foreskin, though he has in fact been circumcised,] may eat terumah, and from their own words [that is, on the basis of rabbinic authority] they decreed [that he should not] because he looks like an uncircumcised male.
   b. They objected [quoting the following teaching]: A man the skin of whose penis has been pulled forward must circumcise [suggesting that he is as though uncircumcised and should therefore not eat terumah, even (we are to assume) according to the Torah].
   c. [This requirement is only] according to the rabbis.

The problem, as understood here, quite clearly is not the failure to perform the mitzvah alone, for we are explicitly speaking of a man who has been circumcised. The problem, rather, is the *appearance* of uncircumcision, as specified in (a). The conclusion of this exchange is that, though according to the Torah such an appearance creates no disability, the rabbis deem even the appearance of a foreskin to be objectionable, and so a person with "pulled skin" must recircumcise.

Before he does, he must not partake of terumah. Of course, the appearance itself might make it appear that the mitzvah has not been performed, so the rabbinic caution is well taken. But one gets the sense that *appearing* as though uncircumcised is of itself the source of rabbinic horror. Given the multiple negative associations hinted at above—associations which, in their combination, detail the contemporary *rabbinic* attitude toward uncircumcision—evidence of such horror should not surprise us.

We will consider one last exchange which rounds out, in a surprising and even shocking way, the rabbinic exercise of categorizing uncircumcision.

a. The master said [quoting a baraita that was already quoted in passing]: A person without distinguishable sexual characteristics [a *tumtum*] may not eat terumah [whereas] his wives and slaves may eat. [A man with pulled skin and one born without a foreskin may eat. A hermaphrodite may eat terumah but may not eat devoted things. A *tumtum* may eat neither terumah nor devoted things.]

b. From where would a *tumtum* have wives? . . .

c. Abbaye said: [We are talking about a case in which] his testicles are evident[8] from the outside [but his penis is nevertheless undescended; since he is evidently a man, he may take wives].

d. Rava said: What is [the actual meaning of] "his wives" [literally: his women]? His mother . . .

e. Come and hear [quoting a part of the above baraita]: A *tumtum* may eat neither terumah nor devoted things.

f. It is fine for Abbaye [that the baraita teaches the law of the *tumtum* twice]; the first teaching speaks of one who is certainly uncircumcised and the latter teaches of one who is possibly [but not definitely] uncircumcised [since, if he/she has a penis, it has not descended from the body cavity nor is it visible from outside],

g. but for Rava [above at d], why does he need the *tumtum* of the latter teaching? [It would be thoroughly redundant.]

h. *What is [the meaning of] tumtum [in this latter statement]? One who is uncircumcised.* [emphasis added]

The immediate task of the final steps of this deliberation (e through h) is to determine whose solution to the earlier problem ("From where would a *tumtum* have wives?"), Abbaye's or Rava's, is correct. As it happens, the baraita in question speaks of the *tumtum* twice, introducing an apparent redundancy into the text. This provides the gemara the opportunity to evaluate the former proposed solutions by asking whether they would help resolve the redundancy problem as well. Typically, the gemara seeks to support the viability of both proffered solutions, but this turns out to be easier in Abbaye's case than in Rava's. To be specific, Abbaye's solution, proposing an unusual interpretation of the first *tumtum* ("his testicles are evident from the outside"), allows for a different reading of *tumtum* in each of its two usages. But Rava's earlier solution, which reinterprets "his women" to mean "his mother," suggests no apparent resolution of the redundancy, so the gemara suggests a solution in his name: What is the meaning of the second "*tumtum*"? One who is uncircumcised.

We should understand that this is a "linguistic" solution, not a technical halakhic one. If the intent were to say that the latter *tumtum* is one who is known to have a foreskin (perhaps because his testicles are evident from outside his body), then this solution would be identical with the one given in Abbaye's name (though now with the order reversed: the former is possibly uncircumcised, the latter is definitely so). But this is impossible because their opinions are clearly presented here as being in opposition. The latter solution, speaking for Rava, must therefore be understood as reinterpreting the second "*tumtum*" to mean "the uncircumcised." This is supported, in fact, in the gemara's next steps, in which a logical problem (we already know that one who is doubtfully circumcised is prohibited from eating; it is therefore obvious—and hence unnecessary to teach—that one who is certainly uncircumcised may not eat) motivates the following rereading of the baraita: "A *tumtum* may not eat terumah because he is possibly uncircumcised [thus far, the first part of the baraita with the gemara's proposed addition] and *one who is uncircumcised* may eat neither terumah nor devoted things." The "*tumtum*" of the baraita is simply replaced, in this rereading, with "the uncircumcised." The term speaks explicitly of one (the person who has unclear sexual characteristics), the gemara suggests that it should be understood as speaking about the other.

What is the gemara assuming when it proposes that the one may represent the other—that (I think it would be fair to understand the gemara this way) the uncircumcised is somehow sufficiently similar to the *tumtum* that one may use one term to represent either? Bear in

mind: the common understanding of the term *tumtum* is not subject
to question. A *tumtum* is, as we have said, one whose sexual characteristics have not made themselves evident. May the same be said
about the uncircumcised male? It seems to me that this is precisely
the equation being offered here. If I understand it correctly, the gemara's claim is that the uncircumcised male, like the *tumtum*, is a person of ambiguous sexual identity. Or, to frame it from the opposite
perspective, the Jewish male is the one with the circumcised penis.
One who is uncircumcised is not only not fully *Jewish* but also not
fully *male*. Circumcision and Jewish maleness are so much tied to
one another in the rabbinic consciousness that it is possible for these
rabbinic authors to argue that the presence of a foreskin obscures the
male identity of the one who has it.[9] In the end, the uncircumcised
Jewish male is not only barely a Jew—he is also, from the Jewish
perspective, barely a male.

The Jewish male is thus defined by what he is not: he is not uncircumcised. But, as the present gemara has shown, he is also (by virtue
of lacking a foreskin) not impure, not foreign, not disgusting, not
dead. He has performed the mitzvah of Abraham and has thus set
himself apart from all of these "other" conditions. He is the Jew, and
the male, in the fullest sense. His circumcised penis is testimony to
this fact.

9.

On Human Suffering

As we have commented on numerous occasions, the Bavli stands at the end of a long and varied tradition. By the time of its composition, the rabbinic community had already produced the Mishnah, the Tosefta, halakhic midrashim on four of the Torah's books, several major aggadic midrashim, and the Yerushalmi. In addition, rabbinic tradents continued to transmit teachings, attributed to sages of the third through fifth centuries, that had not yet found a home in a canonical context. Together, the documentary and traditional record formed a massive foundation on which the writers of the Bavli could build. In fact, in view of their self-perception as inheritors of and successors to that tradition, they had no choice but to build on what their predecessors had transmitted. Thus, though the final voice of the Bavli's authorship contextualizes and shapes everything, the trace of the earlier rabbinic tradition is everywhere to be found in its pages.

For this reason, one of the most important tasks of the Bavli's reader is to evaluate how the Bavli relates to its inherited tradition—to itself, as it were. If meaning resides in difference, then the Bavli's meanings will often emerge from the difference between the voice of its inherited tradition and its own voice. Critique will be found in the reinterpretation or occasional refutation of that tradition. Innovation will be implicit in the Bavli's apparent shift in direction. Conflicting voices will yield tensions whose resolution bespeaks the Bavli's chosen meaning, and forced or apparently difficult interpretations will reveal the Bavli's disquiet with the teaching at hand. Everywhere, therefore, the relationship between the Bavli's analytical voice and the analyzed tradition demands the reader's attention.

To illustrate the points just enumerated, I have chosen what is the Bavli's longest deliberation on the problem of suffering, found at Berakhot 5a-b. This sugya is particularly outstanding for the way it echoes and turns back upon itself, with later comments qualifying or contradicting earlier comments on more than a few occasions. The question that will constantly confront us is, how are we to take these qualifications and contradictions? Are they to be harmonized or allowed to stand in tension? Are we intended to notice the contradictions or difficulties at all? Are we to go along with difficult interpretations or claims of meaning, even if they contradict our sense of the simple meaning of a text?

My proposed answers to these questions depend upon arguments made in chapter 1 of this book. I argued there that the Bavli, like any form of communication, addresses a particular kind of real-and-imagined audience. To begin to make sense of the communication of any given author(ship), one must first determine the nature of the audience addressed and then judge how the chosen forms of communication are likely to be understood by that intended audience. In the case of the Bavli, I suggested, the intended reader is massively literate in biblical and rabbinic tradition. He is questioning and critical. He is confident of his own intellectual resources and willing to use them. He is neither passive nor submissive; Talmud is an active and demanding process, one which demands the reader's critical input at each stage of its deliberation.

Given this picture, it seems likely that the reader is intended to approach a text such as the one examined below with critical sensors fully attuned. He will recognize reinterpretations or contradictions. He will be called upon to evaluate such phenomena and to respond. If reasonable reconciliations are available, he will probably be invited to assent to them—but he will not be asked to suspend critical judgment. Thus, when a text works against itself, it will be his responsibility to evaluate the rhetoric of such a move. And, given his assumed confidence, he will be asked to identify with one position or another, but not without challenging himself with the alternative. The text will never be reduced or simplified; he will always be sensitive to its complexities.

With this in mind, we now turn to the text at hand.

(Transition:)

A. And R. Isaac said: Anyone who reads the Shema upon his bed [that is, upon going to sleep] demons separate from him . . .

B. R. Shimeon b. Laqish said: Anyone who engages in [the study of] Torah, suffering separates from him, as it says . . .

C. R. Yoḥanan said to him, this [idea that you have just expressed] even children in school know it, for it says, "He said, 'If you will heed the Lord your God diligently, doing what is upright in His sight, giving ear to His commandments and keeping all His laws, then I will not bring upon you any of the diseases that I brought upon the Egyptians, for I the Lord am your healer' " (Exod. 15:26).

D. Rather, anyone for whom it is possible to engage in [the study of] Torah and does not [thus] engage, the Holy One, blessed be He, brings upon him ugly, horrible suffering, as it says . . .

I describe this exchange as a transition because the text has not yet devoted its attentions exclusively to the question of suffering; what follows does not speak of suffering but of God's generosity in giving the Torah. The primary emphasis here, therefore, should be understood to be Torah, not suffering. The opinions wish to emphasize the importance of Torah study; suffering is the threat that looms behind the text's exhortation. Suffering is incidental, not central.[1]

Still, this transition serves the following discussion of suffering in two ways. First, it builds the bridge to the primary discussion of suffering; it is the excuse that allows the text to address this central problem. Second, it emphasizes that there is an opinion—that the study and observance of Torah ensures that God will protect the person thus engaged from suffering—that is so obvious that "even the child in the school knows it." As we shall see, when the deliberation below has the opportunity to reflect upon this opinion (from several perspectives, but by implication) it turns out that it is not nearly so obvious as is claimed. Thus, the introduction of this opinion lulls us into a sense of unwitting confidence. It is this sense that the following deliberation will challenge.

I.

A. Rava, and some say R. Ḥisda, said:[2]

1. If a man sees suffering coming upon him, he should examine his deeds, as it says, "Let us search and examine our ways, And turn back to the Lord" (Lam. 3:40).

2. If he searched and did not find [his deeds to be the cause of his suffering], he should attribute it to neglect of Torah [study], as it says, "Happy is the man whom you discipline, O Lord, the man You instruct in Your teaching" (Ps. 94:12).

3. And if he attributed it [to the neglect of study] but did not find [his study to be wanting] then it is clear that they are afflictions [suffering] of [God's] love, as it says, "For whom the Lord loves, He rebukes" (Prov. 3:12).

B. Rava said R. Seḥora said R. Huna said:

1. Anyone whom the Holy One, blessed be He, desires, He afflicts with suffering, for it says, "And the one whom the Lord desires, He crushes with illness" (Isa. 53:10).[3]

2. Is it possible [that this is the case] even if he does not accept them willingly [lit. = "with love"]? Scripture says, "if he made himself an offering for guilt" (ibid.)—[meaning] just as an offering is [offered] willingly, so too suffering [must be accepted] willingly.

3. And if he accepted them [willingly] what is his reward? "He might see offspring and have a long life" (ibid.), and not only so, but his learning will remain with him,[4] as it says, "And that through him the Lord's purpose might prosper" (ibid.).

C. R. Jacob b. Idi and R. Aḥa b. Ḥanina dispute:

1. One says: What is suffering of love? Any [suffering] that does not cause the neglect of Torah, for it says, "Happy is the man whom you discipline, O Lord, the man You instruct in Your teaching" (Ps. 94:12).

2. And one says: What is suffering of love? Any [suffering] that does not cause the neglect of prayer, as it says, "Blessed is God who has not turned away my prayer, or His faithful care from me" (Ps. 66:20).

3. R. Aba the son of R. Ḥiyya b. Abba said to them: This is what R. Ḥiyya b. Abba said [that] R. Yoḥanan said—[Both] these and these are suffering of love, as it says, "For whom the Lord loves, He rebukes" (Prov. 3:12). Rather, what does scripture [mean

when it] says, "the man You instruct in Your teaching?" Don't read "instruct him" [the more literal rendering of this verse] but "[and from your Torah] instruct us," [meaning] this thing You instruct us from your Torah, [that is] a fortiori from [the law of the removal by a master of] the tooth or eye [of his slave]; what if [by the removal of] a tooth or an eye, which are but one of a man's limbs, a slave goes out to freedom, suffering, which cleanses the entire body of a person, how much moreso [should a person "go out to freedom"]!

3A.   And this is [the same as the opinion of] R. Shimeon b. Laqish, for R. Shimeon b. Laqish said: "Covenant" is stated with respect to salt and "covenant" is stated with respect to suffering. "Covenant" is stated with respect to salt, as it is written, "you shall not omit . . . the salt of your covenant" (Lev. 2:13), and "covenant" is stated with respect to suffering, as it is written [following the long recitation of afflictions that Israel will suffer if she does not obey God's will], "These are the terms of the covenant" (Deut. 28:69)—just as with "covenant" spoken of with respect to salt, the salt sweetens the meat,[5] so too with "covenant" spoken of with respect to suffering, the suffering cleanses all of a person's transgressions.

First, it is necessary to clarify the system by which the translation of the text is presented here. It will immediately be evident that I am following a different system than that followed elsewhere. Ordinarily, my divisions of the text are intended to recreate the smallest units of expression, thereby facilitating reference. But here my intent is to delineate what I understand to be the substantive structure of the text, showing where the expression of a single coherent idea leads to the expression of another distinct, coherent idea. Where such expressions subdivide into substantive (not formal) units, I indicate such divisions as well. For example, at I, the statement of Rava (or R. Ḥisda) divides into three distinct ideas: (1) The first response to suffering; (2) the first fall-back position (what if sin, in the normal sense, is not at the root of a person's suffering?); and (3) the final, safety position (if [2] doesn't work, there is still an explanation available). Though each of these statements relates to the preceding one, each could nevertheless be formulated independently with little adjustment and still express a perfectly coherent idea ("If a person suffers, yet neither sins nor neglects Torah study, it must be suffering of love."). In contrast, in I.C., though there are three expressions relating to suffering of love (what is and what isn't), the final opinion (3) is built on a series of individual steps and is then supported (or correlated) with a related opinion, itself built on a series of steps (C.3A.). The point, throughout, is a single one: suffering—apparently (but *only* apparently; see later) and potentially any suffering—is an expression of God's love, because it cleanses one of one's sins and thereby leads to "freedom." To be sure, this idea takes many formal steps to express. But there is a single, basic idea here nonetheless.[6]

Now to the substance of this first part of the deliberation. The overall concern of I. is what the Talmud calls "sufferings of [God's] love." The idea contained in this term is a simple one: as a parent will reprove a child with love, so too will God reprove individuals (see Deut. 8:5, quoted later in this discussion). Suffering has undeniably positive consequences; it should therefore be understood as a good gift from God. The present deliberation seeks to define precisely when suffering can be understood as an expression of God's love. In A., we learn that the more conventional explanation of suffering should be preferred; that is, we should first consider sin as the possible source of suffering. At this point, the suffering of love explanation is seen as a kind of last resort. But in the following steps, suffering of love becomes the exclusive concern of the authorities. In B., it is admitted that some individuals might have trouble accepting the notion that suffering is an expression of divine love. Therefore, the text explains that suffering will only be suffering of love if that suffering is accepted out of love. If it is, then the suffering will lead to great reward. In C., we discover that, in the opinion of some, certain suffering—suffering that leads to a breakdown of communication with God—cannot be suffering of love; if God loved us, why would God remove the possibility of communication? But the final opinion in this section remarks that even such suffering is not to be excluded from the category of suffering of love. Suffering in general is considered, on two accounts (the logical relation to the minor suffering of a slave and the relation of suffering to "covenant"), potentially a manifestation of divine love.

If our sense of the expression of distinct ideas is correct, then this deliberation may be said to exhibit a consistent formal structure. The tripartite expression of ideas, often perceived as characterizing Talmudic expression, predominates.[7] This threefold repetition gives the deliberation a very distinctive voice and, as we shall see, demands that diversions from this pattern be given particular notice. At present, the balance and order of the text create a confident context for the articulation of mostly traditional ideas—those already widely expressed in scripture and earlier rabbinic literature. Supporting the impression of traditionality is the regular reference to scriptural prooftexts. In fact, each of the lessons supported by scripture is relatively straightforward; one is left with the impression that these opinions do, for the most part, indeed reside in scripture. Thus, the voice of biblical tradition looms large. If one were to go no further, this would represent a thoroughly traditional expression.

Yet, this air of confident traditionality is not entirely without qualifications. The first such qualification is the admission, in B., that suffering of love is conditional. Suffering will only be suffering of love if it is accepted out of love, that is, willingly. If there is hesitation or misgiving on the part of the sufferer, then it is not suffering of love. Implicit in this statement, of course, is the recognition that such acceptance might not be easy; as we shall see in the text that follows, even the most pious individuals might not accept suffering. The second reservation is found in the dispute in C. concerning the possible disqualification of certain kinds of suffering from the said category. The reasons for the suggested disqualification are well understood: If you can't speak to God (prayer) or God won't speak to you (through study of Torah) then how can this be suffering of love? Stated in other terms, this disqualification applies to extreme suffering. By insisting on these exceptions, these opinions open up the possibility that certain extreme forms of suffering might go searching for, but not find, a ready explanation. For this reason, we are relieved when the final opinions reject these exceptions. Still, as we shall soon discover, this rejection is a set-up. Even R. Yoḥanan, to whom this opinion is attributed, insists that certain suffering cannot be suffering of love. In retrospect, this easy acceptance will appear ironic indeed.

The next major section of this deliberation begins by quoting a teaching from the halakhic midrashim:

II.
A. It is taught: R. Shimeon b. Yoḥai says: Three good gifts did the Holy One, blessed be He, give to Israel, and all were given only by means of suffering. And what are they?
  1) Torah,
  2) and the Land of Israel,
  3) and the world to come.

A1. From where [do we learn] Torah? As it says, "Happy is the man whom you discipline, O Lord, the man You instruct in Your teaching" (Ps. 94:12).

A2. The Land of Israel? For it says, "the Lord your God disciplines you just as a man disciplines his son," and it is written after it, "For the Lord your God is bringing you into a good land" (Deut. 8:5, 8:7).

A3. The world to come? For it is written, "For the commandment is a lamp, The teaching is a light, And the way to [future] life is the rebuke that disciplines" (Prov. 6:23).

B. 1. A Tanna taught before R. Yoḥanan: Anyone who engages in (1) Torah or (2) deeds of lovingkindness or (3) buries his children, all of his sins are forgiven him.

2. R. Yoḥanan said to him: It is fine with Torah and deeds of lovingkindness, for it is written, "Iniquity is expiated by loyalty [kind deeds] and faithfulness [truth]" (Prov. 16:6)—"loyalty," this is acts of lovingkindness, for it says, "He who strives to do good and kind deeds/ Attains life, success, and honor" (Prov. 21:21); "faithfulness," this is Torah, for it says, "Buy truth and never sell it" (Prov. 23:23). But burying one's children, where is this from?

3. That elder taught in the name of R. Shimeon b. Yoḥai: It is derived by a scriptural equation of "iniquity" and "iniquity"; it is written here, "Iniquity is expiated by loyalty and faithfulness" and it is written there, "but visit the iniquity of the fathers upon their children" (Jer. 32:18).

C. R. Yoḥanan said: Sores and "children" are not suffering of love.

1. And are sores not? But is it not taught: Anyone who has any one of these four appearances of skin ailment, they are none other than an altar of atonement.

   a. They might be an altar of atonement, but they are not suffering of love;

   b. And if you wish I will say: this [the teaching in C.1.] relates to us [in Babylonia, for skin ailments do not disqualify us from anything] and this [R. Yoḥanan's statement] relates to them [for, in the Land of Israel, skin ailments cause certain disqualifications due to impurity];

   c. And if you wish I will say: this [the teaching in C.1.] is [speaking of a case where the skin affliction is] private [in a covered location on the body] and this [R. Yoḥanan's statement] is [speaking of a case where the skin affliction] is public.

2. And are "children" not?

    a. How is this to be imagined? If you say that [we are talking about a case in which] he had them and they died, did not R. Yohanan say "This is the bone of my tenth son!"[8]

    b. Rather, this [R. Yohanan's statement above at C.] is where he did not have them at all and this [his statement here at C.2.a., assumed to support the notion of suffering of love] is where he had them and they died.

I designate this section of text as a single major unit by virtue of the connection of each step with the one preceding it, though the latter step (C.) is not immediately related to the first (A.), that is, beyond the overall theme of suffering of love. So A. is related to B. by the designation of tannaitic authority, by its inclusion of Torah, by its tripartite structure, and by its attribution of the final answer to R. Shimeon b. Yohai (at B.3.), the alleged author of the opinion in A. B. is related to C. in its discussion of "children" and in the difficulty that R. Yohanan has with "children" in both of the steps. Still, I admit that important connections can also be found with the lengthy section that follows, so it is necessary to read these sections together as well as apart from one another.

The first portion of this section is quoted from a lengthy discussion of suffering in the Mekhilta and Sifrei. What may be notable about its present quotation is the omission of the introduction to R. Shimeon's comment as recorded in those midrashim. Unlike here, where the Talmud merely commences by saying, "Three good gifts did the Holy One . . . ," in the midrashim, R. Shimeon's opinion is introduced with the words, "*Suffering is precious*, for three good gifts. . . ." Because in the midrashim the tradition appears in the context of a series of statements that commence with this introductory formula, we might surmise that it was added subsequent to the midrash's formulation under the influence of the larger context. If this is so, then the Bavli's version may be more "original." Alternatively, we could easily suppose that the Bavli merely preserved a slightly different version of this tradition. Therefore, whatever the history of this difference, we might readily suppose that the Bavli's reader could not reasonably be expected to know the midrashic alternative. If not, then the Bavli's present formulation demands no particular attention; suffering is defended, God's goodness (if not justice) is upheld.

However, as we shall see, the question of whether suffering is precious plays a crucial role in the present deliberation. Below, several sages are addressed with the question, "Is suffering precious to you?" (The Hebrew adds only one word to change the affirmative declaration into a question.) Each time the question is asked, the answer is direct and unambiguous: "Neither they [the sufferings] nor their reward!" With this utter rejection of the preciousness of suffering, it is difficult not to wonder whether the midrashic introduction *was* known and *consciously* omitted here. If the reader was familiar with the alternative, the contrasting Bavli version would be notable. Why, he would ask, is the claim "suffering is precious" absent? And he would discover the answer below: the Bavli rejects this notion. Unfortunately, we may never know whether the midrashic expression was part of the active tradition of the Bavli's student. We are forced to say, therefore, that *if* it was, the Bavli's difference is significant.

The second segment of the present text (B.) begins by arguing again on behalf of the benefits of suffering. If these forms of suffering lead to the forgiving of sins, then they must surely be suffering of love. But R. Yoḥanan's response reveals, now more explicitly, that the apologetic for suffering is not as simple as might appear. The problem is that, though R. Yoḥanan can find scriptural support for the claims concerning Torah and deeds of lovingkindness, he allegedly cannot find such support for the claim that the loss of one's children leads to the forgiving of sins. But the reader may well detect multiple signals which will lead her or him to question this failure. First, Yoḥanan's proofs for Torah and lovingkindness require the combination of three verses; the proof for burying one's children requires only two. Second, his successful proofs are original, whereas the proof he fails to offer has already been expressed in the tradition (by R. Shimeon b. Yoḥai). Third, the proof that he fails to supply is given by some anonymous elder; is it possible that the great R. Yoḥanan is unable to find a simple proof when an unnamed elder can? Finally, we learn (at C.2.a.) that there is good reason for R. Yoḥanan to have difficulty with "burying one's children"—he himself was forced to do so and thus he knew this pain intimately. Is it this pain, we are forced to ask ourselves, that doesn't allow him to find scriptural proof for the benefits of losing one's child?

Turning to C., we again see that R. Yoḥanan has misgivings with suffering that involves "children": he is unwilling to admit that it, along with skin afflictions, is suffering of love. Moreover, it appears that the text has misgivings here as well. Unlike all of the traditions that have come before this, R. Yoḥanan's statement is built of two points, not three. Yet we have grown accustomed to the threefold expression, so when we come across this teaching, which disrupts the now-common pattern, we trip. We ask, what is wrong here? Why is this point *different?*

With respect to R. Yoḥanan's dissent on skin afflictions, some equilibrium is quickly recovered: three solutions to the apparent contradiction of his statement with another authoritative teaching are offered. But this recovery only compounds the problem represented in R. Yoḥanan's other dissent—the threefold solution to the "skin ailments" difficulty forces us to notice that the number three appears nowhere in the discussion of children, not in the problem and not in the solution.

Oddest of all is the way that R. Yoḥanan's dissent on "children" is challenged: He can't really mean that " 'children' are not suffering of love" because he was also accustomed to saying "This is the bone of my tenth son." Apparently the gemara is suggesting that, for some reason, this statement should be taken as evidence that the loss of one's child, obviously experienced by R. Yoḥanan himself, is in fact suffering of love.[9] But we ourselves would be tempted to say that for precisely this reason R. Yoḥanan is unwilling to accept such an experience as suffering of love! Would we be impious for arriving at such a conclusion? Are we to concede, despite alternative and possibly better interpretations, that R. Yoḥanan does, in fact, believe that the loss of one's children is suffering of love, as the gemara here demands? Since R. Yoḥanan's statement ("this is the bone") is represented here as deriving from another context, we can only really judge if we consider the context from which it was taken. Fortunately, the Talmud supplies us further on with a context that is clearly more "original," and thus we will be invited to judge for ourselves. It seems to me that, in light of the "original" context, the meaning given to this statement here becomes highly implausible. In my opinion, the author of this deliberation intentionally asks us to reconsider and ultimately to reject his conclusions.[10] At this point it is sufficient to note that there are already several signals, both formal and substantive, that cause us to respond to the gemara's present arguments with misgivings.

Now, in the penultimate section of this deliberation, we are introduced to "the real R. Yoḥanan," and we learn, in the course of this introduction, a great deal about R. Yoḥanan's attitudes toward suffering.

III.
A. R. Ḥiyya b. Abba became ill. R. Yoḥanan went in to him.
1. He said to him: Is suffering dear to you?
2. He said to him: Neither it nor its reward.
3. He said to him: Give me your hand.
He gave him his hand and raised him.
B. R Yoḥanan became ill. R. Ḥanina went in to him.
1. He said to him: Is suffering dear to you?
2. He said to him: Neither it nor its reward.
3. He said to him: Give me your hand.
He gave him his hand and raised him.
(And why? Let R. Yoḥanan raise himself [for we have seen that he has the power to do so in the preceding story]! They say, "One who is imprisoned does not release himself from prison.")[11]
C. R. Eleazar became ill.[12] R. Yoḥanan went in to him. He saw that he was lying in a dark room. [R. Yoḥanan] uncovered his arm and a light fell [over the room] and he saw that R. Eleazar was crying.
1. He said to him: Why are you crying?
a. If it is because of Torah that you have not [studied] sufficiently, we have taught [in m. Menaḥot 13:11], "It makes no difference whether one does much or little, provided that he directs his heart to heaven."
b. And if it is because of food, not every man may merit two tables [wealth].[13]
c. And if it is because of children, *this is the bone of my tenth son* [emphasis added].
2. He said to him: I am crying on account of this beauty that will rot in the earth.[14]
3. He said to him: For this you should surely cry
And the two of them cried together.[15]
4. He said to him: Is suffering dear to you?
5. He said to him: Neither it nor its reward.
6. He said to him: Give me your hand. . . .

In this segment of the deliberation, the present consideration of suffering comes to a climax. The essential point is made in the first two virtually identical sections (A. and B.). When questioned regarding their attitudes toward their suffering, both sages respond by declaring that neither it nor its reward is desired by them. To put it in other words, if this is what is necessary to attain reward, keep it! Both parties would rather be spared the suffering.

The response to suffering modelled in this text is quite startling. To begin with, it is clear that the suffering experienced here is some kind of illness; each sage is confined to his bed, and it is necessary that each be raised (= healed). At the same time, there is no explicit evidence that we are speaking of suffering so severe that it would render the sufferers unable to pray or study—though, to be sure, if we (mistakenly) sought to reconcile this with what came earlier we could insist upon such a reading. Nor, obviously, is the present suffering related to the loss of one's children or to skin afflictions. According to all parties, therefore, this is suffering that might qualify as suffering of love.

But we immediately realize that this cannot be suffering of love because, as we learned earlier (at I.B.2.), to be suffering of love, adversity must be accepted with love, and that clearly is not the case here. Neither, however, can it be deemed suffering of punishment, for these sages actively intercede to eliminate the suffering of the other. If this suffering were understood as God's punishment, there could be no justification for their initiatives.[16] In fact, these masters evidently do not accept that their suffering is the direct will of God at all; if it were, how could they intervene to reverse it rather than recommending repentance? But if it is not the will of God, then what is it? What is it in the attitudes or beliefs of these rabbis that leads them to respond as they do?

Unfortunately, answers to these questions are not readily forthcoming. But certain possibilities are negated, at least, in the more complex final section (C.). Upon discovering R. Eleazar weeping, Yoḥanan asks him why he is doing so. Yoḥanan does not wait for an answer, but instead rejects what he believes to be certain obvious possibilities. If it is because of lack of sufficient study, he says, no problem! It is not quantity that counts but proper intention. Again, R. Yoḥanan works against more conventional opinions expressed much earlier: Lack of sufficient Torah study ("neglect of [study of] Torah" at I.A.2.)

was offered, it will be recalled, as good reason for suffering. Not so, says R. Yoḥanan. Alternatively, if it is because of the lack of wealth conventionally understood as reward from God (its inverse must therefore be punishment), this condition, too, is not to be interpreted in this way. Again, no reason to cry. And, says R. Yoḥanan, if it is because of "children," neither is this reason to cry, for, Yoḥanan points out to Eleazar, "This is the bone of my tenth son."

How are we to understand this last step in R. Yoḥanan's comforting of R. Eleazar? The comment regarding "children" is found in a series of statements regarding what R. Eleazar lacks. He believes that he lacks sufficient Torah and he sees that he lacks wealth. The possible problems are not the loss of something but its absence to begin with. Conversely, when Yoḥanan responds that there is good reason to cry, it is for something that he most assuredly has, his own beauty. The contrast, apparently, is between something now enjoyed and something never possessed. Therefore, it seems likely to this reader that the same is being said about children: lack of children is not something to cry about. Why? Because "this is the bone of my tenth son." In other words, R. Yoḥanan comforts his friend by indicating that things could have been much worse. If he thinks that childlessness is painful, look at the alternative. Far more painful is the loss of a beloved child.

I am arguing for this understanding based upon signals to the reader given in this text alone. It may be objected that R. Eleazar is known in the Talmud to have had at least one son (R. Pedat; see Ber. 11b and M.Q. 20a). However, it seems to me that there is no reason to admit that knowledge here. Matters of family biography are rarely a significant factor in the Bavli's deliberations, so the reader will rarely be called upon to notice (let alone recall) such factors. Therefore, as the reader considers the present deliberation, its own signals will be far more powerful in influencing interpretation than details that might or might not be available elsewhere. Reasonably, we must assume that we have all the information we are intended to have and our present reading must proceed on those grounds alone.

The suggested sense of the text at hand is supported from the most unlikely of places—medieval rabbinic commentators who, as a matter of policy, seek to reconcile contradictory talmudic teachings that appear in scattered locations. I am speaking of the Tosafot, who comment at Nidda 8a (s.v. *"v'amar"*):

> [Commenting on the fact that R. Pedat is identified in this text as being the son of R. Eleazar:] And should you say that in the first chapter of Berakhot [5b, our text here] R. Yoḥanan said to R. Eleazar, "If because of children, this is the bone of my tenth son," *suggesting that R. Eleazar did not have children*, it could be said [in response to this problem] that he was born to him after [this story in Berakhot] or that he had many children and some of them died. . . . [emphasis added]

So Tosafot, too, believe that the clear sense of the present text is that R. Eleazar has no children. Their reading respects what they see as the simple meaning of our gemara, and their preferred reconciliation suggests that R. Pedat must have been born after the events described in Berakhot. Our proposed interpretation therefore gains support: What R. Yoḥanan means to say is that the lack of children is insignificant next to their loss.

This immediate reading has significant implications for our understanding of the earlier segment of the deliberation at II.C.2. If there is no reason to understand R. Yoḥanan's statement as evidence that he believes the loss of children is suffering of love, as now seems clear, then we should finally reject the forced conclusion of that step above. As we have now learned, Yoḥanan grieves the loss of children deeply. It is for this reason that he *rejects* such suffering as "suffering of love"—precisely as we had preferred earlier.

Are we to be troubled by the contradiction between this conclusion and the conclusion expressed explicitly at II.C.2.? I think not. First, we should recall that the very formulation of the text invited us to question the sincerity of its explicit avowal (Why does the threefold structure break down? Why does the gemara fail to supply more than a single forced resolution? Is its failure to "give" to the extent we had grown to expect a consequence of its own misgivings?). Moreover, now the gemara has given us precisely the evidence we need to challenge its earlier claim. It did not need to do so. By supplying this information, the gemara invites us to reread and to reevaluate. We are justified in sensing that the gemara, too, was not fully comfortable with its first tentative interpretation of R. Yoḥanan's bitter statement.

Of (the textual) R. Yoḥanan we now know this: He is extremely bitter about his suffering. He has suffered the loss of a child and he is in no mind to accept such suffering. He would be willing to forgo the reward if he could avoid the suffering. But where, in the opinion of

R. Yoḥanan, is value to be found? What truly is worth crying about? The answer, we see in the final, crucial step of this last exchange (2. through 3.; the final exchange [4. through 6.], if it belongs at all,[17] is a mere formulaic repetition of what has come before), is "this beauty"—the beauty of R. Yoḥanan—that will, with his death, rot in the ground. In the end, it is all reduced to the simple and undeniable beauty of the mundane. Grander conceptions, those which transcend the mundane, are dismissed as being (at the very least) inscrutable or, possibly, without redeeming value. Apologies for God's ultimate justice and the meaning of God's world find no hearing with these masters. As Qohelet (Ecclesiastes) himself might remark, only that which can be definitively grasped has enduring value.[18]

But, almost perversely, this is not the end of this deliberation on suffering. Someone has added a very different conclusion, one that returns us to pieties apparently long put aside (in this context).

IV.
 A. R. Huna, four hundred barrels of wine turned sour on him.
 B. R Judah the son of R. Sala the Pious and the sages (and there are those who say it [was] R. Ada b. Ahava and the sages) went in to him and said: The master should examine his ways [to see if there was any sin that caused this punishment].
 C. He said to them: And am I suspect in your eyes?
 D. They said to him: Is the Holy One, blessed be He, suspected of doing judgment without justice?
 E. He said to them: If there is someone who heard something about me, let him speak.
 F. They said to him: This is what we have heard, that the master has not given vines [due in payment] to his hired man.
 G. He said to them: Is anything left to me from him? He has stolen everything!
 H. They said to him: This is what people say, "The one who steals from a thief tastes the taste [of his theft]."
 I. He said to them: I accept upon myself that I will give it [his due] to him.
 J. There are those who say that [as reward for his "repentance"] the vinegar once again became wine,
 K. and there are those who say that [as reward] vinegar went up in price and sold for the same amount as wine.

The point of this narrative is the same as so many before it: suffering, even of the economic sort, must be punishment for sin. Therefore, the first thing to do when one experiences such suffering is to examine one's ways (B. = I.A.1. above). We have come full circle.

But how are we to respond to this in light of what came earlier in this text? When we hear the question, "Is the Holy One, blessed be He, suspected of doing judgment without justice?" we are tempted to say, "What about R. Yoḥanan and his loss of a child? Was *that* justice? Certainly, R. Yoḥanan was not willing to admit to this."[19] Against the tense struggle with the meaning of suffering that has preceded this, this final piety fails to convince.

Moreover, this final narrative is also formally distinct from the preceding deliberation. Unlike almost everything above, the stamp of tripartite formulation is completely absent from this segment of text. It is difficult to see a triplet in this exchange, even when it is deduced in the most artificial way.[20] So not only the substance of what is said here but also the way in which it is said sets this last section off from the rest.

How are we to understand the inclusion of this story at the end of the lengthy preceding deliberation? Perhaps the text wishes to signal some discomfort with the implications of the earlier discussion and allow the reader to recover more conventional views.[21] But, if this is the intent, the efforts are ironically thwarted. The challenge articulated earlier cannot easily be put behind. Are we being called to take issue with what came before? This seems to me unlikely. In my reading, the contrast that the placement of this story has highlighted only calls into question the assumptions upon which it is built. Which is more powerful, after all: the lengthy, detailed struggle represented in the earlier deliberation, or the conventional conclusions offered here? If this represents a retreat from the more radical statements that have come earlier, it has (in this immediate context) ultimately failed. If, instead, the intent is to invite us to compare and contrast the opinion with which we began—repeated here again—with those opinions we have encountered in the course of deliberation, then this has been accomplished brilliantly. As we return to this position at the end, we *are* forced to ask whether it can be upheld against the bitter rejections heard earlier. At the very least, after following R. Yoḥanan through his personal struggle with suffering, no reader can be sure that this final, very ancient opinion is one that he or she can fully accept.

Finally, it is the sense of struggle that emerges most resoundingly from this lengthy deliberation. The problem of suffering and the question of its meaning are difficult, perhaps too difficult—as the very difficulty of this text precisely illustrates. Having worked through the various approaches to the problem, we are left with no obvious solutions. And we might well be correct in concluding that that very point—the absence of solutions—is precisely what this text and its author wanted to communicate.

10.

The Difference a Lens Makes

W hat difference does a lens make? To answer this question, I now turn to other readings of texts I have read above, seeking to illustrate how different choices—different guesses concerning the genre of the text at hand—yield radically different conclusions.

I begin with Jacob Neusner's reading of the sugya examined in chapter 3 (B.Q. 83b–84a). In his ongoing work on the Bavli, Neusner's operative assumption (his "genre guess") has been that the Bavli is a Mishnah commentary. Not surprisingly, his reading of the present sugya supports this assumption/conclusion is all of its details. Neusner's immediate comments on the text at hand are these:

> I.1, glossed by No. 2, bearing its own little talmud at Nos. 3–4 [all in my I.], provides scriptural bases for both the premises and the rules of the Mishnah paragraph. Nos. 5–13 [my II. and following] continue the sequence of proofs begun at No. 1, each bearing its contraindication as well.[1]

Later, in his outline of this text, Neusner briefly describes the manner in which each teaching demonstrates that "eye for eye" means monetary compensation, suggesting that such a demonstration is the fundamental point of this talmudic passage.[2]

What this gemara is about, in Neusner's opinion, is providing the scriptural basis for the Mishnah's law. One way or another, it is true,

a scriptural basis for the law can be found in this extended deliberation. Hence, Neusner's designation of gemara as "mishnah-
commentary"—in which commentary means, among other things,
identifying a scriptural source for the rabbinic law at hand—draws
attention to an aspect of gemara with which we might readily concur.
Furthermore, Neusner does note that a number of the steps include
"contraindications," though he doesn't explain what this means nor
does he suggest what the purpose of such "contraindications" in a
commentary might be. Still, if the gemara is "commentary"—by
definition—then contraindications surely belong in a commentary
(yes, this is circular). For those predisposed to see commentary, the
proof that the gemara is commentary will not be hard to identify.

But, in my opinion, the genre-definition of gemara as commentary
falls short in important respects. To begin with, for such a definition
to be instructive, it is necessary to compare gemara with other texts
which are commonly assigned to the genre "commentary." The gemara is, in obvious and significant ways, different from the *Anchor Bible
Commentary* or the *New Jewish Publication Society Torah Commentary*. It is different from commentaries on Shakespeare or Homer. It
is even different, again, in obvious and significant ways, from well-
known commentaries on the Mishnah—say, that of R. Ovadiah of
Bertinura, or Ḥanokh Albeck. What, then, do we mean by a "commentary?" In what ways does the gemara fit common definitions of
commentary and in what ways does it not? Most importantly, what is
the meaning of the gemara's differences? What is the significance of
its not-commentary qualities? Before the genre definition can be of
value, these questions require answers.

By reading the Talmud not as commentary but as literature, we
have noticed and accounted for elements of the Bavli's rhetoric the
commentary lens seems not to see at all. We have noticed, first, the
way many of the gemara's approaches highlight the weaknesses of proffered proofs. The rhetorical point of such a move in a work defined as
deliberative literature I have taken to be straightforward: the gemara
means to highlight the tenuous connection of the Mishnah's law to
scripture. What can be the purpose of such undermining in a commentary? Second, we have seen that the gemara refutes fully half of
the proofs at hand. If the rhetorical point is, as I have said, to show
the weakness of the connection between the Mishnah's law and scripture, then these refuted proofs will readily find a place in the overall

rhetorical scheme. If this is a commentary, though, then why include such rejected proofs at all? Why not simply quote those proofs which successfully ground the Mishnah's law in scripture, as such a commentary would presumably seek to do? Third, we have seen that several of the accepted proofs seem forced or contrived—easily understood in my literary analysis, but difficult to understand if the point is commentary. Fourth, we have seen that the final opinion (that of R. Eliezer, who says that "eye for eye" means just that) accepts the more literal meaning of scripture and requires no forced interpretation. Moreover, when the gemara tries to explain this opinion away, it misreads R. Eliezer's chosen wording and makes claims that border on the ridiculous ("Doesn't R. Eliezer accept all of the above tannaim?" Remember, the gemara itself has not done so!). All of this can be understood if the gemara wants us to recognize how reasonable R. Eliezer's opinion is—and how, in comparison, the Mishnah's law is, scripturally speaking, unreasonable! The "commentary" reading barely seems to notice this rhetoric, let alone to account for it.

None of this is to say that the Talmud is not a commentary. There are certainly important features of the Talmud which do seem to function as commentary, and some texts will more naturally be categorized as commentary than others. But reading the Talmud with a literary lens brings to focus elements of the Talmud's rhetoric that other approaches fail to grasp, and accounts for these rhetorical elements in ways that are promising and suggestive. For this reason, I prefer to read the Talmud as literature.

Many—probably most—readers of the Talmud through the ages have chosen to read the text through what we might call a halakhic lens. The point of reading the Talmud as halakha (rabbinic law) is to extract the established law from the Talmud's deliberations. A representative halakhic reading of the text just reviewed is that of R. Menaḥem HaMeiri (thirteenth century Provence). HaMeiri first explains the law of the Mishnah, accounting for relevant discussions in related gemaras. He then writes:

> This is the explanation of the Mishnah, and it is all, in the fashion that I explained it, the accepted law. . . . From what we have explained, you learn regarding what is said in the Torah, "eye for eye" and also "hand for hand" and everything like it, that the intent is not literally an eye or literally a hand but, rather, monetary compensation. Lest you

say, even "life for life" is meant to be taken literally—scripture says
"don't take ransom for the life of a murderer" . . . for a murderer you
do not take ransom but you do take ransom [monetary compensation]
for limbs, even if they do not heal.

What is remarkable about this reading is, first, its great brevity.
Most of the deliberation we examined is irrelevant for purposes of the
halakha and therefore provokes no comment. If a part of the gemara
does not affect the halakhic outcome, the reader who employs this
lens barely sees it. Second, HaMeiri asserts that the Mishnah's law
captures the correct reading of the related scriptural verses. He para-
phrases the one proof from the gemara which apparently strikes him
as most reasonable or convincing, ignoring entirely the problems with
this proof, which the gemara explores in detail. But such explorations
are apparently unimportant. What is important, in such a reading, is
establishing the law and, where possible, showing its source.

Such a reading does, it is true, highlight one important quality of
the gemara at hand: the weight of the gemara's discussion certainly
supports the law as recorded in the Mishnah. HaMeiri effectively reiterates this fact and shows one way this conclusion might be supported.
But his focus on halakha and halakha alone leaves him with little else
to say on a gemara such as this. Why, then, does the gemara take two
pages to say what, in HaMeiri's rendering, takes but a brief paragraph?
If the gemara is "halakha," then why does it suggest nine proofs of the
Mishnah's law, five of which fail? Again, if they fail, why include
them? Perhaps more powerfully, if the point is halakha, why quote
more than one successful proof? As HaMeiri shows, with such a concern, a single proof suffices. In fact, a single proof is better, because an
additional proof force us to ask what was wrong with the one before it.

In my reading, all of these halakhically irrelevant details have a
point. Since, in reading the Talmud as literature we need not assume
that halakha is the central purpose of any given text, we are free to
imagine a wide variety of possible meanings and purposes. These may
be halakhic, theological, ethical, or (as yet) unclassifiable. But a literary reading will, by definition, attend to the entirety of a text's formulation and will thus find meaning where the halakhic lens will not. It
seems to me that the Bavli's authors must have had a purpose in composing two lengthy columns (in the Vilna edition) of deliberation and
debate concerning the relationship of the Mishnah's law to scripture.

The halakhic reading fails to account for this immense effort. The literary reading at least stands a chance of succeeding.

I offer here a second example contrasting the commentary and literary readings. Following his translation of Ḥagigah 10a through 11b (chapter 4 above, relating to the Mishnah that enumerates those laws which "hover in the air," "hang from a hair," or "have something [in scripture] on which to depend"), Neusner comments that this gemara

> provides an unusually clear example of talmud as Mishnah-commentary, pure and simple. Readers will have noticed numerous instances in which a single program of exegesis extends through sizable composites of commentaries to discrete sentences or even paragraphs of Mishnah.

What this "single program of exegesis" might be is not clear, but immediately above Neusner describes units of gemara which "add a Tannaite complement to the Mishnah-sentence . . . comment on the allegation of the Mishnah . . . continue the exposition of the Mishnah's language . . . challenge the allegation of the Mishnah . . . [and] continue the systematic, uniform glossing of the Mishnah-statements."[3] Presumably, all of these are things that a commentary would do, so the single program of the Talmud, again, as exemplified here, must be to constitute a commentary.

But seeing this Talmud as commentary doesn't allow the reader to see the finer points of the composite—the rhetoric that resides in more precise elements of formulation. For example, the gemara responds in essentially the same way ("They are written!") to all of the Mishnah's parts, *despite the fact that the Mishnah itself distinguishes three categories!* What is the point of this leveling? Why would a commentary want to undermine the very categories the text upon which it comments constructs? In my reading, this rhetorical leveling seeks to level the fundamental distinction between Written and Oral Torahs. What would be the meaning of such a rhetorical tack in a mere commentary? We also saw that the "exceptions" to the claim that "they are written" turn out to be central to each of the categories of law discussed, thus undermining the very claim being made. In my reading, these weighty exceptions are intended to emphasize that it makes little difference whether a law is written (in Written Torah) or not. Again, we must ask, what is the point of these weighty exceptions in a commentary? Last, we saw (p. 58) that, in one of its sections, the gemara records a tradition ("skin afflictions and tents have little scripture and many laws") which is so absurd as to invite immediate rejection. As I understood it, reference to such an indefensible teaching serves to undermine the Mishnah categories that employ the same now-problematic criteria; again, the erasure of categories! The Talmud's program, this literary reading tells me, is to erase categories and to suggest the fundamental equality of the Written and Oral Torahs. In the later centuries of the development of classical rabbinism, a time when the rabbis were free for the first time to assert their own authority with full confidence, such a program makes sense. If, instead, we read the Talmud as mere commentary, we cannot do justice either to the text's rhetorical complexities or to the messages these features may carry.

With respect to the halakhic reading, my observations regarding HaMeiri's comments above could be repeated here virtually verbatim. In his clarifications of the Mishnah, HaMeiri refers to relevant brief sections of the gemara, even noting when the gemara seems to be in conflict with the Mishnah (the Mishnah says that the law concerning the release of vows "flies in the air"; the gemara insists that there is a scriptural source). But each such reference is brief and pertains to the clarification of the Mishnah. When he comes to this gemara, HaMeiri has almost nothing to say. Again, the gemara's deliberation has few, if any, consequences for the halakha. The halakhic reader therefore finds nothing of note to read.

A third approach to reading the Bavli, claiming numerous modern day adherents, is what may roughly be described as the "source-critical" approach. This method is best represented by the critical commentaries of David Halivni, though we could also turn to the work of Shamma Friedman for a fine example of this sort of reading. As I understand his work, Halivni views the Talmud as its own genre. This genre, "talmud," is characterized by sources that have been transmitted over numerous generations and located, finally, in an interpretive matrix composed by unnamed "editors" or "redactors." To reduce this to a definition: I think it would be correct to say that, in Halivni's opinion, Talmud is an edited or redacted composite of sources and interpretive connectors. Given this genre definition, Halivni is predisposed to see the Talmud as a conglomeration of disparate sources with complex histories (again, circularity!). The histories of these sources are replete with error and misunderstanding (sources are either misquoted or misinterpreted in generations subsequent to their formulation) and, by recovering the history, Halivni is able to resolve problems he detects in the Talmud's final formulation.

The consequences of reading the Talmud with this lens are readily illustrated. In his comments on Yevamot 13b through 14a (my chapter 6), Halivni also notices the difficulty with the objections following the opinions of Abbaye and Rava. These sages, you will recall, propose that different practices in the schools of Hillel and Shammai do not transgress the prohibition "don't make factions" because this prohibition does not apply to different practices in different cities. Therefore, when the gemara objects by referring to stories of different rabbis following different practices in different places, it is difficult to understand the problem. Indeed, even the gemara itself goes on to say, "What is the problem? We have already said that different places are different [and permissible]!" Halivni's solution to this evident difficulty is to suggest that "the objector" disagrees with Abbaye and Rava (whose opinions he may not even have known) and believes that the prohibition "don't make factions" applies even in different cities.[4] In other words, Abbaye and Rava are one source, the objections are another, and the responses to the objections represent still another;[5] otherwise, the "responders" would not have tried to reconcile the objections with the opinions of Abbaye and Rava. Simply put, in Halivni's reading, the author of the latest voice in this exchange misunderstood the relationship of the earlier voices. He thus sought to reconcile what was not meant to be reconciled.

There are surely methodological objections to this solution. For example, no linguistic or other factor obviously distinguishes the voice of the "responder" from the voice of the "objector." On what basis, then—other than our desire to resolve a subjective difficulty—do we make these into different sources? That being said, it is certainly possible to construct a history of the gemara text that supports such a solution and, though not demonstrable, Halivni's reconstruction is neither impossible nor objectively unreasonable.

My difficulty with Halivni's "source" reading is not what it does but what it does not do—that is, it does not read the Talmud as a final composite whole and seek to make sense of that composite finality. To illustrate the difference between Halivni's approach and the one I propose: Following the second objection (aa), the gemara asks (ee) how R. Abbahu could have followed different practices in different places, given that his attendant might have become confused. The gemara answers, simply, that "he informed his attendant." In my discussion of this text, I asked what possibly could have motivated the inclusion of these two steps. R. Abbahu's attendant had not been mentioned up to this point, and there is certainly no reason that any reader would naturally have asked such a question. I ventured to say that the purpose of this apparently superfluous addition was to introduce us to the "he informed him" solution, a solution which would also be employed further on in the text. Later, you will recall, the gemara insists that the schools of Shammai and Hillel did act on their opinions and yet continued to intermarry, despite the fact that mamzers could result from certain such unions. The gemara explains this liberality by suggesting that "they informed them" when there were potential problems. Of course, given the earlier "superfluous" exchange, this solution was already known by the reader. As a consequence, what might have been a grave problem (different marriage practices) was not a problem at all (it is not a problem if you already know the solution!). In my interpretation of the sugya as a whole, the very point of the Bavli here is to diminish problems with "factions" and permit the widest latitude of practices within observant Jewish communities. For this reading, the voice of the "respondent" is essential to the dynamics of the sugya. For the source-reader, on the other hand, this same voice is merely misguided, and irrelevant beyond its place at the end of the textual history.

I reiterate that there is nothing impossible in Halivni's reading. But such an approach to reading does not, in my opinion, do justice to the Bavli as we preserve it, and I therefore prefer the literary approach I have outlined and illustrated in earlier chapters. Mine, as all others, is a chosen lens. But it is a lens that, in my sensibility, captures the Talmud text more completely. It seeks not to break the text apart and to privilege some of its parts over others, but to read it together and to hear the nuances of its final formulation. The alternatives now stand before you, the reader. You, obviously, will decide for yourself.

A Parable

The ancient rabbis were sitting, composing what they called a Talmud. A question arose: How should we read the Torah? Is it best to understand it literally, heeding the command of every detail, or is there room for flexibility in interpretation? Before them the rabbis had records of earlier, more authoritative teach-ings, some of which supported one view and some another. What should they do? How should the Torah be read?

Their ruling came down: "It is a dispute of tannaitic sages," they said. This dispute would stand. No ultimate decision would be made. (See b. Sanh. 45b.)

As I have said, the choice of one lens or another has important conse-quences. The meaning of a text—what it says to us, what it demands of us—will be profoundly affected by this choice. Yet we need not decide upon a single lens, a single approach to reading. On the con-trary, we should live with indecision and, as did the Talmudic rabbis, even respect it. Our various readings, side by side, will enrich our understanding and appreciation of the text at hand. To borrow from a well-known Talmudic maxim: "The rest is commentary; go and read."

Notes

Chapter 1

1. See Rabbi Irwin H. Haut, *The Talmud as Law or Literature* (New York: Bet Shaʿar Press, 1982).

2. Avraham Weiss, *Ha-yetzirah ha-sifrutit shel ha-amoraim* (New York: Horeb Yeshiva University, 1962).

3. *Semeia: An Experimental Journal for Biblical Literature* 27 (1983).

4. Louis Jacobs, *Structure and Form in the Babylonian Talmud* (Cambridge, Eng.: Cambridge University Press, 1991). Though I agree with many of Jacobs's scattered assertions, I am sorry to say that I think this is a particularly weak volume, with no sense of method whatsoever.

5. René Wellek and Austin Warren, *Theory of Literature*, 3d ed. (San Diego: Harcourt Brace Jovanovich, 1977), p. 23.

6. Terry Eagleton, *Literary Theory: An Introduction* (Minneapolis: University of Minnesota Press, 1983).

7. Ibid., pp. 7–8; emphasis in original.

8. All of the present quotations of Eagleton are found on p. 9.

9. Northrop Frye, *The Great Code: The Bible and Literature* (New York and London: Harcourt Brace Jovanovich, 1982).

10. Ibid., pp. 53 and 59–60.

11. *Anatomy of Criticism* (Princeton, N.J.: Princeton University Press, 1957 [repr. 1971, 1973]), p. 315.

12. See Ellen Schauber and Ellen Spolsky, *The Bounds of Interpretation:*

Linguistic Theory and Literary Text (Stanford: Stanford University Press, 1986).

13. See E. D. Hirsch Jr., *Validity in Interpretation* (New Haven and London: Yale University Press, 1967), pp. 19, 40.

14. Ibid., p. 86.

15. Exemplary studies have been collected in Sanford Levinson and Steven Mailloux, eds., *Interpreting Law and Literature: A Hermeneutic Reader* (Evanston, Ill: Northwestern University Press, 1988).

16. The exception is Shamma Friedman. But his primary concern, too, is source-critical, and he is ultimately more interested in the "original" meanings of the Talmud's sources than in the meanings and motivations of the final formulation.

17. Owen M. Fiss, "Objectivity and Interpretation," in *Interpreting Law and Literature*, p. 229.

18. Roy Kreitner, "Reading Tradition, Writing Scripture," in *New Perspectives on Ancient Judaism*, vol. 5, *Society and Literature in Analysis*, ed. by Paul Virgil McCracken Flesher (Lanham, MD: University Press of America, 1990), p. 118.

19. This is not to say that the authors of the Bavli did not hope to create a "classic," one that would be studied by successive generations of readers for many centuries. It is only to admit that the Bavli's authors were unlikely to have imagined that subsequent readers would significantly differ from their contemporary reader.

20. Kreitner, pp. 118–19.

21. Stanley Fish, *Is There a Text in This Class?* (Cambridge, Mass.: Harvard University Press, 1980), pp. 344–45.

Chapter 2

1. See David Kraemer, "The Formation of Rabbinic Canon: Authority and Boundaries," *Journal of Biblical Literature* 110, n. 4 (1991): 619.

2. Several manuscripts lack "on Shabbat."

3. This sentence (or its equivalent) is absent in MS Munich. As it stands, the Munich version makes no sense, and it seems likely, therefore, that these words were omitted in error by the scribe.

4. According to b. Meg. 31a, the whole book of Jonah is to be read as the haftara during the afternoon service of Yom Kippur. In later practice, the whole book of Obadiah is read as the haftara for the Sabbath portion *va-yishlaḥ*.

5. See the opinion of Eugène Dupréel, quoted in Chaim Perelman and Lucie Olbrechts-Tyteca, *The New Rhetoric: A Treatise on Argumentation* (Notre Dame and London: University of Notre Dame Press, 1969), p. 55.

6. Jacob Neusner, *Midrash in Context* (Philadelphia: Fortress Press, 1983), pp. 135–36.

Chapter 3

1. This part of the verse, though present in the Vilna edition, is missing in manuscripts. Its presence or absence does not affect the sense of the text.

2. In MS Munich the text has here merely "and it is written." The precise method of midrash changes according to this reading but not the fundamental point.

3. The next brief section of the sugya, as recorded in the printed editions, is missing in several manuscripts. Tosafot, s.v. "*af haka^cah*," object to its inclusion for logical reasons. In any case, its presence changes little the overall thrust of the present steps and, for that reason, I omit quotation or comment.

4. A quick counting shows that this is offered as an explanation for the formulation of a Mishnah or baraita in excess of seventy-five times. By contrast, the same explanation is applied to scripture only approximately a dozen times.

5. Halivni, in a radical source-critical move, does just this, suggesting that the original teaching is "It comes 'For' 'For.' " See *Meqorot umesorot: Baba Qamma* (Jerusalem: Magnes Press, 1993), p. 314.

Chapter 4

1. See Jacob Neusner, *Judaism: The Evidence of the Mishnah* (Chicago: University of Chicago Press, 1981), p. 277.

Chapter 5

1. The Yerushalmi's version, at the end of Ḥagigah chap. 1, is this: "Scripture, Mishnah, Talmud, laws and narratives—even that which an experienced student will one day teach before his master—was already spoken to Moses at Sinai."

2. Also at b. Sotah 47b and Sanh. 88b.

3. An Aramaic word that, like "Meir," derives from the root for "light." Alt.: Meisha; see *Diqduqei soferim*, ad loc.

4. That is, R. Judah the Patriarch. Alt.: Rav; see *Diqduqei soferim*, ad loc.

5. Alt.: Rav or Rava; cf. Sanh. 17a and *Diqduqei soferim* here.

6. See *Diqduqei soferim*, ad loc.

Chapter 6

1. The preceding phrase does not appear in all versions of the Mishnah.
2. R. Solomon Aderet records the following variants in his commentary:

> z1. You might have thought that . . . it is like two courts in one city.
> z2. You might have thought that . . . it is like one court in one city.

According to z1, the gemara suggests that the objection was originally directed against Abbaye's interpretation of the "don't make factions" prohibition. According to z2, it was directed even against Rava's.

3. On this point, see D. Halivni, *Meqorot umesorot: seder nashim.* (Tel-Aviv: Dvir, 1968), pp. 15–17. Halivni notes: "The ordering of these objections after the statements of Abbaye and Rava doesn't work well" (p. 15), and suggests that the person who originally raised these objections didn't know the opinions of Abbaye and Rava. Yitshak Gilat reaches a similar conclusion; see *"lo titgodedu," Bar-Ilan* Annual 18–19 (1981):83 (in Hebrew).

4. Given the larger rhetorical picture of the Bavli, I would venture that such questions are often more important than they at first appear.

5. The phrase appears a total of only 124 times in the entire Bavli, and only eight times in Yevamot.

Chapter 7

1. I have translated according to the printed version, which follows Rashi's emendation. For the more original reading, see my comments below.

2. See Tosafot, s.v. *"batefilla"* and *Diqduqei soferim* ad loc.

3. Rashi and other medieval commentators suggest that the distinction is that Shema is a scriptural commandment, whereas prayer is a rabbinically ordained ritual. However, neither this Mishnah nor this gemara hint at such a distinction and there is no reason for us to believe that one is assumed at this point.

4. This is the apparent explanation of the step at hand. But see D. Halivni, *Meqorot umesorot: seder nashim,* (Tel-Aviv: Dvir, 1968), pp. 655–56.

5. In the printed edition and MS Oxford, the sense of "entirety" is communicated through an emphatic repetition: *"kol hatorah kulah."* The latter term is absent in MS Munich. The sense is not changed, however, because the gemara still speaks of *"kol hatorah"*— "the whole Torah."

Chapter 8

1. The point is made pertaining to definitions in general by Saussure and others following him; see Terry Eagleton, *Literary Theory: An Introduction*

(Minneapolis: University of Minnesota Press, 1983), p. 97. In his study of category formation, George Lakoff suggests the association of categories and language in general; see *Women, Fire, and Dangerous Things: What Categories Reveal about the Mind* (Chicago: University of Chicago Press, 1987), chap. 6. Lakoff's reflections on the present point are found at pp. 576–8.

2. See Lakoff, chapters 4 through 6.

3. Most manuscripts have here "R. Eliezer."

4. Rashi's quotation of the gemara includes what is here marked in brackets. It is also added in the margin of a manuscript in the Vatican collection. In any case, the gemara demands of the reader—and it can rightly be expected of the reader—that he know the entirety of the verse and read it into the context here.

5. See previous note.

6. See D. Halivni, *Meqorot umesorot: Eruvin-Pesahim* (Jerusalem: The Jewish Theological Seminary of America, 1982), pp. 535–36.

7. See Tosafot, s.v. "ʿarel."

8. Some records of this gemara lack the term "are evident," and change the text to: "when his testicles are outside [but not his penis]."

9. Anthropologists have noted the association in some cultures of fleshiness and femaleness; see Peter Metcalf and Richard Huntington, *Celebrations of Death* (Cambridge, Eng.: Cambridge University Press, 1991), pp. 114–15. Perhaps the rabbis are here making the same association: the extra fleshiness of the foreskin may be understood to make the penis more female.

Chapter 9

1. I emphasize this point because Louis Jacobs, in his very different outline of this sugya, lists these comments as the first steps of the sugya on suffering. For the reasons just articulated, I do not view them as part of the sugya proper. Jacobs admits that the step that intervenes between those just quoted and what follows "has not connection at all with the theme of sufferings" (p. 33) and he omits it from his outline of the sugya (p. 40), but does not justify on literary grounds his doing so. For Jacobs's analysis of this text, see "The Sugya on Sufferings in B. Berakhot 5a, b," in *Studies in Aggadah, Targum and Jewish Liturgy in Memory of Joseph Heinemann*, edited by Jakob J. Petuchowski and Ezra Fleisher (Jerusalem: Magnes and Hebrew Union College Press, 1981), pp. 32–44.

2. Better: "Rava said R. Seḥora said R. Huna said." See *Diqduqei soferim*, ad loc.

3. Translated for context.

4. Here I follow Jacob Neusner's translation.

5. Or, "causes the sacrifice to cleanse"; see the various alternatives recorded in *Diqduqei soferim*.

6. Louis Jacobs's analysis of this text ignores important substantive and literary characteristics of the text as a whole. For example, though he lists the replies to one objection to an opinion of R. Yoḥanan (below, II.C.1.a–c) as one of his steps (no. 13), he omits the reply to another objection (below, II.C.2.b). What is the difference? Why count one but not the other? I invite the reader to compare my analysis with his. Nevertheless, I support Jacobs's overall argument that this text requires careful literary analysis and I agree wholeheartedly with his claim that "we do not have here a simple anthology of teachings on sufferings, but a carefully thought-out pattern" ("The Sugya on Sufferings," p. 41).

7. See, in particular, Shamma Friedman, *Pereq ha-isha rabba bebavli*, passim. See also David Halivni, *Meqorot umesorot: seder nashim* (Tel Aviv: Dvir, 1968), pp. 271–2, and, on this same sugya, Louis Jacobs, "The Sugya on Sufferings in B. Berakhot 5a, b":40–42. I make it clear elsewhere in my notes in this chapter that I consider Jacobs's imposition of tripartite structuring on all parts of this sugya to be forced and artificial.

8. The version in MS Munich is this: And are "children" not suffering of love? But did not R. Yoḥanan say. . . .

9. Rashi suggests this logic: "A great man like R. Yoḥanan would not be visited by suffering that is not [suffering] of love." Tosafot suggest, in contrast, that "since R. Yoḥanan was accustomed to comfort others with this [that is, by producing the bone of his tenth son], we should learn from this that [he thought that] they were sufferings of love." I strongly prefer the second explanation, first, because Rashi forces us to ignore the fact that, as Tosafot point out, "many righteous individuals have had no children," despite the gemara's conclusion here that infertility is not suffering of love, and, second, the gemara below supplies an "original" context for R. Yoḥanan's comment in which his clear intent is to comfort another with his act.

10. The sort of reading demanded by this text (by any text, I would argue, but particularly here) is well articulated by Steven D. Fraade, in *From Tradition to Commentary* (Albany: SUNY Press, 1991), p. 125.

11. MS Munich begins with the story of R. Yoḥanan (B) and then, to make the point that R. Yoḥanan should raise himself, refers back to an as yet untold story of R. Yoḥanan's healing of R. Ḥiyya b. Abba. Other versions also differ in various details. These differences eliminate the complete structural balance of the present text but do not affect the substance of the discussion in any essential way.

12. The printed text has Eliezer, a common error.

13. Tosafot offer this reading in place of "no man merits two tables" for obvious reasons. The original version, rejected by Tosafot, is supported by MS Munich and several other records of this text. See *Diqduqei soferim*.

14. Manuscripts make it clear that the intent is to "your beauty," that is, the beauty of R. Yoḥanan.

15. This narrative statement and the exchange that follows, identical with preceding exchanges, are missing in MS Munich and certain versions. See *Diqduqei soferim.*

16. As evidence that the Bavli recognizes this connection, see Ber. 60a, bottom.

17. See n. 15.

18. I cannot for a moment agree with Jacobs's suggestion that these steps are intended to be humorous ("The Sugya on Suffering," p. 44). There is nothing humorous about suffering or in the deliberation on it in this text. Its striking him as humorous can only be on account of the immense irony of the skepticism it expresses.

19. Even the author of the Tosafot on this page (s.v. "*dina*") is brought to voice such a protest. In his words, "There are many righteous people who are afflicted both in their bodies and their property!" So much for justice.

20. Jacobs manages to find a triplet, but only, as I have said, in the most artificial way; see his outline at p. 41 of "The Sugya on Sufferings." He leaves out numerous steps from the narrative (the initial suggestion that Huna examine his ways, the statement by his interlocutors of the sin of which he is suspect, and so on) without any rhyme or reason. He is merely forcing the text into his preconceived schema.

21. Jacobs calls this a "happy ending" (ibid., p. 42).

Chapter 10

1. Jacob Neusner, *The Talmud of Babylonia: An Academic Commentary* 20, *Bavli Tractate Baba Qamma* (Atlanta: Scholars Press, 1994), p. 367.

2. Ibid., pp. 616–18.

3. Jacob Neusner, *The Talmud of Babylonia: An Academic Commentary,* XII, *Hagigah* (Atlanta: Scholars Press, 1994), pp. 40–41.

4. See *Meqorot umesorot: seder nashim* (Tel-Aviv: Dvir, 1968), pp. 15–16.

5. Halivni suggests as much in n. 1, p. 15.

Bibliography

Boyarin, Daniel. *Intertextuality and the Reading of Midrash*. Bloomington: Indiana University Press, 1990.

Eagleton, Terry. *Literary Theory: An Introduction*. Minneapolis: University of Minnesota Press, 1983.

Fish, Stanley. *Is There a Text in This Class?* Cambridge, Mass.: Harvard University Press, 1980.

Fiss, Owen. "Objectivity and Interpretation." In *Interpreting Law and Literature*. Edited by Sanford Levinson and Steven Mailloux. Evanston, Ill.: Northwestern University Press, 1988.

Fraade, Steven D. *From Tradition to Commentary*. Albany: SUNY, 1991.

Friedman, Shamma. *Pereq ha-isha rabba bebavli*. Jerusalem and New York: Jewish Theological Seminary of America, 1977.

Frye, Northrop. *Anatomy of Criticism*. Princeton: Princeton University Press, 1957 [repr. 1971, 1973].

———. *The Great Code: The Bible and Literature*. New York and London: Harcourt Brace Jovanovich, 1982.

Goodblatt, David. "The Babylonian Talmud." In *Aufsteig und Niedergang der römischen Welt* II, vol. 19.2. Reprinted in *The Study of Ancient Judaism* II. Edited by Jacob Neusner. Hoboken, N.J.: Ktav Publishing House, 1981.

Green, William Scott. "What's in a Name? The Problematic of Talmudic 'Biography.' " In *Approaches to Ancient Judaism: Theory and Practice*. Edited by W. S. Green. Missoula, Mont.: Scholars Press, 1978.

Halivni, David. *Meqorot umesorot: Baba Qamma.* Jerusalem: Magnes Press, 1993.

———. *Meqorot umesorot: eruvin-pesahim.* Jerusalem: The Jewish Theological Seminary of America, 1982.

———. *Meqorot umesorot: seder nashim.* Tel Aviv: Dvir, 1968.

———. *Meqorot umesorot: yoma-hagiga.* Jerusalem: The Jewish Theological Seminary of America, 1975.

———. *Midrash, Mishnah and Gemara: The Jewish Prediliction for Justified Law.* Cambridge and London: Harvard University Press, 1986.

Haut, Irwin H. *The Talmud as Law or Literature.* New York: Bet Sha'ar Press, 1982.

Hirsch, E. D., Jr. *Validity in Interpretation.* New Haven and London: Yale University Press, 1967.

Jacobs, Louis. *Structure and Form in the Babylonian Talmud.* Cambridge, Eng.: Cambridge University Press, 1991.

———. "The Sugya on Sufferings in B. Berakhot 5a, b." In *Studies in Aggadah, Targum and Jewish Liturgy in Memory of Joseph Heinemann.* Edited by Jakob J. Petuchowski and Ezra Fleischer. Jerusalem: Magnes and Hebrew Union College Press, 1981.

Kraemer, David. "Composition and Meaning in the Bavli." *Prooftexts* 8, n. 3 (1988):271–91.

———. "The Formation of Rabbinic Canon: Authority and Boundaries." *Journal of Biblical Literature* 110, n. 4 (1991):613–30.

———. "The Intended Reader as a Key to Interpreting the Bavli." *Prooftexts* 13, n. 2 (May 1993):125–40.

———. *The Mind of the Talmud: An Intellectual History of the Bavli.* New York: Oxford University Press, 1990.

———. "On the Reliability of Attributions in the Bavli." *Hebrew Union College Annual* 60 (1989):175–90.

———. *Responses to Suffering in Classical Rabbinic Literature.* New York: Oxford University Press, 1995.

———. "The Rhetoric of Failed Refutation in the Bavli." *Shofar* 10, n. 2 (Winter 1992):73–85.

Lakoff, George. *Women, Fire, and Dangerous Things: What Categories Reveal about the Mind.* Chicago: University of Chicago Press, 1987.

Levinson, Sanford, and Steven Mailloux, eds. *Interpreting Law and Literature: A Hermeneutic Reader.* Evanston, Ill.: Northwestern University Press, 1988.

Metcalf, Peter, and Richard Huntington. *Celebrations of Death.* Cambridge, Eng.: Cambridge University Press, 1991.

Muilenberg, James. "Form Criticism and Beyond." *Journal of Biblical Literature* 88 (1969):1–18.

Neusner, Jacob. *Judaism: The Evidence of the Mishnah*. Chicago: University of Chicago Press, 1981.

———. *Judaism: The Classical Statement*. Chicago and London: Chicago University Press, 1986.

———. *Midrash in Context*. Philadelphia: Fortress Press, 1983.

———. *Reading and Believing: Ancient Judaism and Contemporary Gullibility*. Atlanta: Scholars Press, 1986.

———. *The Talmud of Babylonia: An Academic Commentary*. Atlanta: Scholars Press, 1994.

———. *Talmudic Thinking: Language, Logic, Law*. Columbia: University of South Carolina Press, 1992.

Perelman, Chaim, and Olbrechts-Tyteca, Lucie. *The New Rhetoric: A Treatise on Argumentation*. Notre Dame and London: University of Notre Dame Press, 1969.

Rabbinovicz, R. *Diqduqei soferim*. 2 vols. New York: M. P. Press, 1976.

Schauber, Ellen, and Ellen Spolsky. *The Bounds of Interpretation: Linguistic Theory and Literary Text*. Stanford: Stanford University Press, 1986.

Stern, David. *Parables in Midrash: Narrative and Exegesis in Rabbinic Literature*. Cambridge, Mass.: Harvard University Press, 1991.

Vizotsky, Burt. *Reading the Book*. New York: Doubleday, 1991.

Wellek, René, and Austin Warren. *Theory of Literature*, 3rd ed. San Diego: Harcourt Brace Jovanovich, 1977.

Index